MW01009967

ISBN 978-1-934655-30-6

06-021 • COPYRIGHT © 1986 **World Evangelism Press**®
Revised 2008
P.O. Box 262550 • Baton Rouge, Louisiana 70826-2550
Website: www.jsm.org • Email: info@jsm.org
225-768-7000
All rights reserved. Printed and bound in U.S.A.
No part of this publication may be reproduced in any form or by any means
without the publisher's prior written permission.

TABLE OF CONTENTS

CHAPTER   **PAGE**

A Study In Bible Prophecy

The Cross Of Christ Series

Chapter 1

The Rapture Of The Church

CHAPTER ONE

THE RAPTURE OF THE CHURCH

The Rapture of the Church of Jesus Christ is the next great event on the horizon of time (perhaps the greatest in all of history). What a glorious event this will be! Millions of people will suddenly disappear from this Earth to rise through the air, past the clouds, to meet their Lord and Saviour in the air.

> *"In a moment, IN THE TWINKLING OF AN EYE, at the last trump: for THE TRUMPET SHALL SOUND, and the dead shall be raised incorruptible, and WE SHALL BE CHANGED.*
>
> *"For this corruptible must put on incorruption, and this mortal must put on immortality.*
>
> *"So when this corruptible shall have put on incorruption, and this mortal shall have put on immortality, then shall be brought to pass the saying that is written, Death is swallowed up in Victory"* (I Cor. 15:52-54).

Is it any wonder that in Scripture it is called . . .

> *"that Blessed Hope"* (Titus 2:13)?

This mass disappearance of the Saints of God is called in Biblical terminology the Rapture of the Church. Although the word *"rapture"* does not appear in the Scripture as such, the fact is clearly taught. Jesus referred to this event when He said:

> *"Let not your heart be troubled: you believe in God, believe also in Me.*
>
> *"In my Father's House are many mansions: if it were not so, I would have told you. I GO TO PREPARE A PLACE FOR YOU.*
>
> *"AND IF I GO AND PREPARE A PLACE FOR YOU, I WILL COME AGAIN, AND RECEIVE YOU UNTO MYSELF; that where I am, there you may be also"* (Jn. 14:1-3).

In other Passages Jesus referred to the *"raising"* of the dead at the Resurrection (Jn. 6:39-54; 11:24; 12:48). The Angels consoled the Disciples of Jesus at His Ascension by referring to the fact that . . .

"THIS SAME JESUS, which is taken up from you into Heaven, SHALL SO COME IN LIKE MANNER as you have seen Him go into Heaven" (Acts 1:11).

The Apostle Paul spoke of this event as a great *"mystery"* — that is *"something previously hid but now revealed"* (see I Cor. 15:51) — and as being . . .

"caught up together" (I Thess. 4:17).

In Hebrews it is referred to as *"translated"* (Heb. 11:5).
These few Scriptures could be multiplied in regard to the teaching of the Rapture of the Church.

DEFINITION OF TERMS

One of the central, Biblical Texts for the teaching of the Rapture is as follows:

"Then we which are alive and remain shall be CAUGHT UP together with them in the clouds, to meet the Lord in the air: and so shall we ever be with the Lord" (I Thess. 4:17).

The words *"caught up"* come from a Greek word *harpazo,* meaning to *"carry off,"* to *"grasp hastily,"* to *"snatch up."* Our English word *"rapture,"* being the equivalent of the Greek *harpazo,* denotes *"being possessed by an overwhelming emotion* (such as joy, love), *ecstasy, or wild excitement."* As such, it is a most appropriate word to use in describing this glorious event. Certainly it will be a time of wild excitement and great joy when the Lord appears and we are caught up to meet Him in the air to be with Him forever. No wonder that the next Verse exhorts us:

"Wherefore comfort one another with these words" (I Thess. 4:18).

Now, there are two other words used in the Scriptures that relate to the Rapture. The first of these two words is found in the following Verse:

"Now we beseech you, Brethren, by the COMING of our Lord Jesus Christ, and by our GATHERING together unto Him" (II Thess. 2:1).

The word *"coming"* is translated from the Greek word *parousia*, which means *"an arrival and presence with."* It is used in relation to Christ's arrival both *for* His Saints at the Rapture and *with* His Saints at the Second Coming. Here it signifies not only His Coming for the Saints, but also His Presence with them until His Revelation and Manifestation to the world seven years later.

Another word found in this Verse and used in conjunction with the Rapture is the word *"gathering."* The Greek word is *episunagoge* and means *"a complete gathering"*; that is, of all the dead in Christ and all the living in Christ from all parts of the Earth out of all Denominations and Dispensations to meet Christ in the air. The word literally means *"a gathering together upon."* By extension, it is a separation of the godly living from the ungodly.

The second word that refers to the Rapture is found in the following Verse:

> *"And now, little children, abide in Him; that, when He shall APPEAR, we may have confidence, and not be ashamed before Him at His Coming"* (I Jn. 2:28).

The word *"appear"* comes from the Greek word *phaneros* and means *"to appear"* in the sense of revealing one's true character: The same word is used later by John:

> *"Beloved, now are we the sons of God, and it does not yet APPEAR what we shall be: but we know that, when He shall appear, we shall be like Him; for we shall see Him as He is"* (I Jn. 3:2).

Think of that! The Word tells us that at the Rapture not only does Jesus reveal to us His True Nature, but at the same time our true nature is also revealed. Only those who have become . . .

> *"partakers of the Divine Nature"* (II Pet. 1:4)

. . . will recognize Him. This is the *"mystery"* that Paul spoke of when he said:

> *"Behold, I show you a mystery; WE SHALL NOT ALL SLEEP, BUT WE SHALL ALL BE CHANGED,*
> *"IN A MOMENT, IN THE TWINKLING OF AN EYE, AT THE LAST TRUMP: FOR THE TRUMPET SHALL SOUND,*

*AND THE DEAD SHALL BE RAISED INCORRUPTIBLE,
AND WE SHALL BE CHANGED.*
*"For this corruptible must put on incorruption, and this
mortal must put on immortality"* (I Cor. 15:51-53).

Many other Scriptures relate to the fact of the Rapture and the man-
ner in which it will take place; for example, (Lk. 21:34-36; Jn. 14:1-3;
I Cor. 15:23, 51-58; II Cor. 5:1-8; Eph. 5:27; Phil. 3:11, 20-21; Col. 3:4;
I Thess. 2:19; 3:13; 4:13-17; 5:9, 23; II Thess. 2:1, 7-8; James 5:7-8;
I Pet. 5:4; I Jn. 2:28; 3:2).

DIFFERING VIEWPOINTS

There are many and diverse opinions on the subject of whether the
Church of Jesus Christ will be present here on Earth during the Great
Tribulation or whether the Church will be *"raptured out"* and escape
the Tribulation altogether. As is the case in the other areas of Biblical
interpretation, many compelling arguments can be made for each position, and each can be supported to a greater or lesser degree somewhere
in Scripture. Several of the more prominent viewpoints on the Rapture
may be singled out here for specific mention.

NON-RAPTURE. Many modernists have completely rejected any
concept of a Rapture. And these Denominations, in their repudiation of
literal interpretation of Scripture, have completely suppressed any con-
sideration of our Lord Jesus Christ's Return physically to reign as King of
kings and Lord of lords. It is not surprising, therefore, that they also
reject the idea that His Church will rise to meet Him in the clouds at the
time of His Return.

PRE-TRIBULATION RAPTURE. We who adhere to this view believe that the Lord will return to Earth approximately seven years prior
to His Return to the Mount of Olives to assume His Throne. At this time,
He will remove His Church from the world so that it will escape completely
the Great Tribulation outlined in Revelation, Daniel, and other Scriptures.

MID-TRIBULATION RAPTURE. Those who support a Mid-Tribulation Rapture believe that Jesus will return for His Church, but they
time the event somewhere around the midpoint of the seven-year Tribulation Period.

POST-TRIBULATION RAPTURE. Bible scholars of this school
of thought contend that the Church will remain here on Earth for the
Great Tribulation, after which its survivors will . . .

"rise . . . to meet the Lord in the air"

. . . and land (along with the dead in Christ) upon the Mount of Olives where they shall . . .

"ever be WITH THE LORD" (I Thess. 4:16-17).

Much attention has been focused on these questions, and volumes of teachings abound on all shades of opinions and manner of viewpoints. There is growing support within the Christian community for the argument that if the Church is going to be taken out, and a person has made plans to go through the Great Tribulation, he will have lost nothing by preparing himself for this eventuality. On the other hand, if the Rapture is not to take place before the Great Tribulation, and he has not prepared for it, he stands to lose everything. While this is logical, it is also *faithless*. It seems the Christians who accept this view are, in effect, looking for punishment. This view supposes that the Church needs to experience the Wrath of God to be purified.

We cannot support this theory. We cannot see a great and loving God pouring out His Wrath upon His own Children — Children bought and adopted through the Power of His Son's Blood shed at Calvary.

SCRIPTURAL SUPPORT FOR A
PRE-TRIBULATION RAPTURE

First, Jesus said that the Saints will escape the *"things that shall come to pass"*; viz., the Great Tribulation.

"And take heed to yourselves, lest at any time your hearts be overcharged with surfeiting, and drunkenness, and cares of this life, and so that day come upon you unawares.
"For as a snare shall it come on all them who dwell on the face of the whole Earth.
"Watch ye therefore, and pray always, that you may be accounted worthy to ESCAPE ALL THESE THINGS that shall come to pass, and to stand before the Son of Man" (Lk. 21:34-36).

The *"things"* that we shall escape are given in Matthew, Chapter 24; Luke, Chapter 21; and Revelation, Chapters 6 through 19.

1. WAR;

2. FAMINE;

3. DEATH;

4. RELIGIOUS PERSECUTION;

5. EARTHQUAKE;

6. SIGNS AND WONDERS IN THE HEAVENS;

7. HAIL, FIRE, AND BLOOD;

8. SEA AND RIVERS TURNED TO BLOOD;

9. FALLING STARS;

10. SUN, MOON, AND STARS DARKENED;

11. DEMONS LOOSED UPON EARTH;

12. SCORCHING SUN;

13. DENSE DARKNESS;

14. DEMONS WORKING MIRACLES; AND,

15. SATANIC DECEPTION.

Second, we are assured that the Saints will escape the Wrath of God.

"For GOD HAS NOT APPOINTED US TO WRATH, but to obtain Salvation by our Lord Jesus Christ" (I Thess. 5:9).

"For the Lord Himself shall descend from Heaven with a shout, with the voice of the Archangel, and with the Trump of God: and the dead in Christ shall rise first:
"THEN WE WHICH ARE ALIVE AND REMAIN SHALL BE CAUGHT UP TOGETHER WITH THEM IN THE CLOUDS, to meet the Lord in the air: and so shall we ever be with the Lord.
"Wherefore comfort one another with these words" (I Thess. 4:16-18).

The exhortation is to receive comfort from these words and to comfort others, but we cannot do that by telling them that they are going through a terrible, horrible wrath first. Can a person have a real, vibrant, assuring, joyous Salvation if he does not have the assurance that he is a Child of God and that he is going to spend eternity in Heaven? Of course not. Neither can a person have a joyous, vibrant assurance of that *"Blessed Hope"* if he knows that he has to go through a Great Tribulation before he attains it.

Third, we are assured that the Church as a body of Believers will escape the Wrath of God.

> *"And now you know what withholds that he might be revealed in his time.*
>
> *"For the mystery of iniquity does already work: ONLY HE WHO NOW LETS WILL LET, UNTIL HE BE TAKEN OUT OF THE WAY.*
>
> *"And then shall that Wicked be revealed, whom the Lord shall consume with the Spirit of His Mouth, and shall destroy with the brightness of His Coming"* (II Thess. 2:6-8).

What hinders the powers of darkness from having full sway today? What prevents the powers of darkness from revealing the Antichrist at this time?

There are three forces that impede the revelation of the Antichrist: (1) governments, (2) the Holy Spirit, and (3) the Church. The hindering cause mentioned here has to be one of these three sources.

Obviously, the governments of the world will not be removed from the Earth because eventually they will become even more prominent during the Tribulation Period. Governments will not really hinder the Antichrist; they will, in fact, aid and abet his program.

The Holy Spirit certainly will not be taken out of the world during the Great Tribulation, because Revelation 7:9-17 establishes that multitudes of people will be Saved during this period. John 3:5-8; Romans 8:9; and Ephesians 2:18 attest that no man is Saved except through the Ministry of the Holy Spirit.

Acts 2:17-21 also clearly states that during the Great Tribulation, the Holy Spirit will be present on Earth. We are well aware that some persons believe (and teach) that the Holy Spirit will be removed. But prayerful reading of these (and other) Scriptures should confirm that this is not the case.

So, with two of the three hindering causes present during the Great Tribulation, we must assume that it is the third source of restraint that will be removed just prior to the Tribulation. What is this hindering cause? Why, the Church, of course! So, it is the Church that will be taken out of the way — raptured . . .

> *"then shall that Wicked be revealed"*

. . . who is the Antichrist.

Fourth, from Revelation, Chapter 4 through Revelation, Chapter 19, we observe a marked change in God's Attitude toward mankind. It changes from Mercy, which has been expressed for thousands of years to that of Judgment. The Body of Christ is not seen on Earth at this time while Judgment is being poured out upon sin and iniquity.

Absolutely nothing is said about the Church on Earth after Revelation 4:1. The Church is mentioned one time in Heaven, but not on Earth.

One group referred to during this time and perhaps mistaken to be the Church is Israel. Jacob is a reference to Israel, and comment is made about *"Jacob's trouble"* (Jer. 30:7). The Great Tribulation will be a time of great trouble for Israel and also for a God-forsaken world. Israel will be brought to a place of national Repentance.

The Wrath of God is not intended to bring the Church into submission. So, the next great event on the horizon of time will be the Rapture of the Church, the Body of Christ. Nobody knows the time of the Rapture, but we do know it will take place before the Tribulation Period.

PURPOSE OF THE RAPTURE

There are many reasons for the Rapture taking place. We shall briefly outline some of these for further study.

1. TO RESURRECT THE DEAD IN CHRIST, THEREBY SEPA-RATING THEM FROM THE WICKED DEAD. This will be the first great Resurrection (I Cor. 15:51-55).

2. TO TAKE THE SAINTS TO HEAVEN where their works will be judged, where they will receive their rewards, and where they will partake of the Marriage Supper of the Lamb (II Tim. 4:8; Rev. 19:9).

3. TO TRANSFORM THE BODY OF THE SAINTS FROM A STATE OF MORTALITY TO ONE OF IMMORTALITY because . . .

   "this corruptible must put on incorruption, and this mortal must put on immortality" (I Cor. 15:53) . . .

   "there shall be no more death, neither sorrow, nor crying, neither shall there be any more pain" (Rev. 21:4).

4. TO PRESENT THE SAINTS BEFORE GOD THE FATHER TO BE WITH HIM FOREVER (Rom.14:11-12).

5. TO MAKE THE SAINTS WHOLE IN SPIRIT, SOUL, AND BODY.

"And the very God of Peace Sanctify you wholly; and I pray God your whole spirit and soul and body be preserved blameless unto the Coming of our Lord Jesus Christ" (I Thess. 5:23).

6. TO CAUSE THE SAINTS TO ESCAPE THE GREAT TRIBULATION AND THE COMING WRATH AND TO STAND BEFORE THE SON OF MAN (Lk. 21:36).

7. TO REMOVE THE HINDERER OF LAWLESSNESS; that is, to get the Church out of the world.

    "For the mystery of iniquity does already work: only he who now lets will let, until he be taken out of the way" (II Thess. 2:7).

8. TO REVEAL THE ANTICHRIST (II Thess. 2:8).

SIGNS OF THE TIMES

Jesus said that just as the sky gives signs of inclement or fair weather (Mat. 16:2-4), just as nature gives evidence of something to come (Lk. 21:30), so the Endtime will be marked by signs of the coming storm. Although some of these events ultimately will take place before the Second Coming of Christ, that many are already occurring reveals the nearness of the Rapture. Some of the signs we are told to look for are as follows:

1. WARS AND RUMORS OF WARS (Dan. 9:26; Mat. 24:6).

2. RESTORATION OF ISRAEL AS A NATION (Ezek., Chapt. 37). Since 1948 the world has been closely observing the miraculous preservation of the tiny Nation of Israel from their sworn enemies who had vowed to exterminate them. God had already given them tremendous victories against astounding odds in the 1948 and 1956 wars. But in 1967 with Russian-trained and Russian-supplied armies, the Arabs once again were sent to annihilate Israel. In June, 1967, outnumbered forty to one, the small ill-equipped Israeli army totally defeated the combined armies of Egypt, Jordan, and Syria. In less than three hours of the first day of the war, Israeli fighter planes destroyed 300 of Egypt's 340 planes — a Miracle of Miracles! Can it not be obvious to anyone that God has miraculously preserved the Nation of Israel since her restoration in 1948?

3. MATERIAL AFFLUENCE (Lk. 17:27-30; II Pet. 2:6-7).

4. SPIRITUAL APOSTASY (II Jn. Vss. 7-11).

5. OVERPOPULATION (Gen. 6:11-13; Mat. 24:36-44). Already the world is bulging with over 6.4 billion people, and there is speculation about how many people the Earth can support. Within a decade that figure could be near 7.0 billion. Such numbers pose real problems for the Earth's natural resources.

6. INCREASED KNOWLEDGE AND TRAVEL (Dan.12:4). No age has seen the speed with which man currently travels and communicates. One of two families changes residence every five years. Telephones and telexes and satellites carry instant communication. Rockets travel to outer space. The speed of this age is unparalleled.

7. NATURAL DISASTERS (Mat. 24:7). Every week, it seems, we hear of earthquakes, storms, tidal waves, or some other calamity occurring somewhere on the globe. Who has ever known of so many volcanic eruptions or so many ecological problems? Truly ours is a unique age.

8. PERILOUS TIMES (II Tim. 3:1-5). Our nation was stunned when President John F. Kennedy was assassinated November 22, 1963, followed by the assassination of Civil Rights leader, Martin Luther King Jr., April 4, 1968, and then the assassination of Senator Robert F. Kennedy by Sirhan Sirhan on June 5 of the same year. Fear, a sense of peril, it seems, came upon the American people. Things were not safe anymore. Even though we were not at war, we were scared. And now we have experienced September 11, 2001, and the ensuing wars in Afghanistan and Iraq.

9. LAWLESSNESS (Jude, Vss. 17-19). And added to that has been the more recent scourge of terrorism worldwide. We cannot walk our streets at night; we cannot leave our doors unlocked; we cannot board an airplane without wondering if some mad gunman might be aboard. We fear for the safety of our home and family. Is it any wonder if we are more uptight than our forefathers, more restless, less at peace? No age has experienced the insecurity and turmoil we are facing today.

10. FALSE PROPHETS (Mat. 24:11-12, 24). Recent best sellers on this subject have made us aware of the subtle deception of so-called Christian prophets. Many have been deceived and will continue to be led astray.

11. ANTICHRISTS (Mat. 24:5). Many false messiahs have appeared, claiming to be Christ; but we know there is only One, and this same Jesus is coming again (Acts 1:11).

12. WICKEDNESS (Mat. 24:12). During the 1960's people began to turn their attention to the fact that we may be living in the Last Days — and indeed we are! Civil disobedience and riots were the order of the day. It seemed that a moral dam had broken loose. Overnight, it seemed, there was a total collapse of morals. There was a flood of legalized pornography, nude obscene performances on stage and movies, wife-swapping, topless entertainers, coed dormitories, skyrocketing divorce rates, sexual promiscuity and introduction of the pill, rock festivals accompanied by all kinds of open sexual immorality and drugs, communal living, rampant venereal disease, the burning of draft cards and the American flag, the popularity of anti-war songs, wholesale deserters from the armed forces . . . and all this with the endorsement of the liberal clergy. The liberal clergy believed that God was acting in all this. Radicals who should have been tried for treason became our national heroes.

13. DEMONIC ACTIVITY (I Tim. 4:1-3). When the Bible speaks of the fierceness of the Wrath of God or His fierce Anger, it uses a word meaning *"burning."* But when it speaks of the fierceness of the demonic activity or wickedness, it uses words characterizing *"vehemence, harshness, danger, and savagery."* This will be the spirit of this age.

14. PERSECUTION OF THE SAINTS (Mat. 24:9). Believers dying as a testimony for their Faith is nothing new in this world. Every age has had its martyrs. It is estimated that millions of martyrs are buried in the Catacombs . . . that in 1900, approximately 36,000 people laid down their life for Christ . . . that in 1970, approximately 230,000 people died for their Faith in Christ . . . that in 1986, approximately 330,000 followed Christ in martyrdom. How many since then?

15. DRUGS (Rev. 9:21; 18:23). Many people are surprised to learn that drug abuse is mentioned in the Bible. No, the word *"drug"* is not used, but another word meaning *"drug"* is used; that is, the Greek *pharmakeia,* translated *"sorcery."* When the word is used, it means *"magic."* But when it applies to drugs, drug use, and the druggist, a form of *pharmakeia* is used. The Bible says that in the Endtime men will give themselves to drug abuse. Has any age

ever witnessed such a fulfillment of this as we are seeing today?

16. SPREAD OF THE GOSPEL (Mat. 24:14). Through literature and telecommunications the Name of Jesus Christ is going forth into all the world.

"But I say, HAVE THEY NOT HEARD? YES VERILY, THEIR SOUND WENT INTO ALL THE EARTH, and their words unto the ends of the world" (Rom. 10:18).

What nation in the world, at some point, in its history, has not heard the Gospel? Jesus said:

"So likewise you, when you shall see all these things, know that it is near, even at the doors" (Mat. 24:33).

That word *"near"* does not mean *"soon"* or even *"immediately."* It is the Greek word *eggus,* meaning *"at hand, nigh unto, ready."* The verb form means *"to draw nigh or to come nigh."* It means *"imminent"* or the next thing on the agenda. All these things either are being fulfilled or have been fulfilled. All things are *"ready."* We believe, then, that Christ could return for His People at any moment.

"Watch therefore: for you know not what hour your Lord does come.
"Therefore BE YOU ALSO READY: FOR IN SUCH AN HOUR AS YOU THINK NOT THE SON OF MAN COMES" (Mat. 24:42, 44).

"Be you therefore ready also: for the Son of Man comes at an hour when you think not" (Lk. 12:40).

LEVITY CONCERNING THE RAPTURE

In the late 1960's a timely book appeared on the scene that was to popularize the teaching of the Rapture. This book was followed by numerous books, movies, and posters. The Rapture was exploited to its fullest both religiously and securely. *Time* magazine carried two references to the Rapture during the epic summer of 1969, and again in June, 1971, their cover story was titled *"Jesus Is Coming Again."*

The word *"rapture"* became the joke of secular entertainers and talk-show hosts. Bumper stickers, billboards, and tracts appeared everywhere carrying references to the *"great snatch."* One such bumper sticker read:

"WARNING: If the Rapture takes place this car will be out of control."
Other catch phrases such as *"the elevator ride in the sky," "the fantastic space voyage,"* and *"the ultimate trip"* became popular overnight.

Within a few years a *"Rapture cult"* had appeared among the Fundamental and Pentecostal Churches. The whole impetus of the Rapture was distorted into little more than being caught up in the *"great snatch."* Preachers jumped on the bandwagon and began to capitalize on the teaching to get people *"in."*

Although there is a great need for a revival of the teaching of the imminent Return of the Lord Jesus Christ in the air for His Saints, there is a greater need for a revival of that *"Blessed Hope,"* which is a purifying Hope. The Rapture of the Church is not to be relegated to a shallow *"snatch."* Every Preacher, every Child of God, will be held accountable for the levity in which he approaches this most serious subject. It is no joking matter when millions of people will be left behind to face the Wrath of God. It is our responsibility to warn the wicked to . . .

> *"flee from the wrath to come"* (Mat. 3:7)

. . . and to prepare the Saints for that any-moment Return of the Lord Jesus Christ to claim His Blood-bought and Blood-washed sons and daughters. It will be an awesome event for those individuals left behind, but a glorious event for those who have prepared themselves for their departure.

A certain amount of levity must have preceded the Flood of Noah's day. The Bible refers to the people eating and drinking (in other words, going about their daily routine) as if nothing were about to happen (Mat. 24:37; Lk. 17:26). Noah preached Righteousness (II Pet. 2:5), apparently without success, because only Noah and his family were saved from the destruction that came upon the whole Earth (Gen. 7:23). Jesus said that as it was in Noah's day, so would it be in the Last Days — people disbelieving or making light of the Wrath of God.

Millions of sincere, but misguided, people have been disillusioned into thinking that they are going to be included in that great *"elevator ride to the sky."* That there will be a Rapture, the Bible leaves little doubt. Who is going to be included in the Rapture is the question. Let us, therefore, approach this most important subject by discussing, first, two Biblical prerequisites for inclusion in the Rapture: (1) to be *"in Christ"* and (2) to be *"accounted worthy."*

IN CHRIST

> *"For the Lord Himself shall descend from Heaven with a*

shout, with the voice of the Archangel, and with the Trump of God: and the dead IN CHRIST shall rise first" (I Thess. 4:16).

According to the above-stated Scripture, the only prerequisite for inclusion in the Rapture is to be *"in Christ."* The same expression *"in Christ"* is used also in II Corinthians 5:17, where Paul investigated the qualities of a man professing to be *"in Christ."*

"Therefore if any man be IN CHRIST, he is a New Creature [literally a New Creation]*: old things are passed away; behold, all things are become new."*

Unfortunately, many readers mistake this simple Scripture to mean that if a person merely *"believes"* in God and Christ, he is therefore *"in Christ"* and thus assured of a place in the Rapture. If this were so, Satan and every demon in Hell would also be included in the Rapture . . .

"You believe that there is One God; you do well: the devils also believe, and tremble.
"But will you know, O vain man, that Faith without works is dead?" (James 2:19-20).

. . . and we know this is not going to be the case. Satan and all his wicked henchmen do believe in God. So, obviously, more is required than mere assent.

Let us look a little deeper into the word *"believe,"* for a correct belief will place a person *"in Christ."*

Many people pin their Hope for Salvation on John 3:16. This, of course, is one of the most significant of all Scriptures.

"For God so loved the world, that He gave His Only Be-gotten Son, that whosoever BELIEVES in Him should not per-ish, but have Everlasting Life" (Jn. 3:16).

A superficial reading of this Scripture and avoidance of a deeper study of its implications seemingly imply that belief is an end in itself. But if belief (in its simplest interpretation) is all that is required, what about James 2:19 mentioned earlier?

That Satan and his helpers will not be Saved (Rev. 20:10, 15) makes it clear that *"belief"* (within the basic dictionary definition of *"being convinced of the reality of something"*) is not by itself sufficient quali-fication for Salvation and inclusion in the Rapture. Then, what is implied in *"believing"* as the term is used in John 3:16 and elsewhere?

The word *"believes"* comes from the Greek verb *pisteuo* and is used almost exclusively in the Gospel of John (some fifty-two times), whereas the word *"faith"* (Greek, *pistis*) is not found in the Gospel of John at all. The Apostle Paul used the word *"faith"* almost exclusively, whereas John used the word *"believe."* Both words signify *"a total reliance on, a trusting in, and clinging to"* as correctly indicated in the *Amplified Bible.*

John's use of the word *"believes"* is more than a mere mental assent; it is rather the total commitment of a man's whole being toward Jesus Christ as the Son of God. The outcome of *"believing"* in Jesus as the Christ, the Son of God, will decide every other moral and spiritual decision in a person's life. This could be summed up briefly by stating that a person who *"believes"* in Christ commits his whole being — body, soul, and spirit — into the life and teaching of Jesus. Just as some parents try to live out their life in their children, the persons who believe in Christ as the Son of God allow Him to live His Life in and through them.

> *"He who has the Son has Life; and he who has not the Son of God has not Life"* (I Jn. 5:12).

The word *"life"* comes from the Greek word *zoe,* meaning *"that quality of life which is derived from God and which characterizes the Personality of Jesus Christ and of those who come to God through Him."* To have the Son means to have the same moral and spiritual quality of life as that of Christ. This is illustrated further:

> *"He who believes on the Son HAS EVERLASTING LIFE: and he who believes not the Son shall not see LIFE; but the Wrath of God abides on him"* (Jn. 3:36).

It is obvious, then, that a person who *"has the Son"* *"believes"* (trusts in, relies on) the Son. Believing is sharing in the Life of Christ, which is imparted to an individual the moment he believes that Jesus is the Son of God, the One Who died for him. To refuse to *"believe"* is to reject or disobey that Life, which Jesus the Son of God came to give us (Jn. 3:16), and, consequently . . .

> *"the Wrath of God abides* [remains] *on him"* (Jn. 3:36).

He is, therefore, condemned . . .

> *"because he has not believed in the Name of the Only*

Begotten Son of God" (Jn. 3:18).

He prefers . . .

> *"darkness rather than light"* (Jn. 3:19).

These Verses prove, without a doubt, the prior statement that to *"believe"* is to commit one's whole being to Jesus Christ as the Son of God. Believing is not a passive acknowledging that Jesus is the Christ; it is an active sharing in the Life of Christ.

> *"HE WHO HAS THE SON HAS LIFE"* (I Jn. 5:12).

This is not an option. God paid a tremendous price for our Reconciliation and Restoration to that Life for which we were originally intended.

> *"God . . . now commands all men every where to repent"* (Acts 17:30).

As *"Ambassadors for Christ,"* and since God is speaking to us in this writing . . .

> *"we pray you in Christ's stead, be ye reconciled to God"* (II Cor. 5:20).

Not only does *"believing"* place an individual *"in Christ,"* but a natural consequence of being *"in Christ"* is to follow Him. Jesus said to the Jews:

> *"I told you, and you believed not: the Works that I do in My Father's Name, they bear witness of Me.*
> *"But you believe not, because you are not of My Sheep. . . .*
> *"MY SHEEP HEAR MY VOICE, and I know them, AND THEY FOLLOW ME:*
> *"And I give unto them Eternal Life"* (Jn. 10:25-28).

Obviously, there was a dramatic difference in the reaction of the Jews who conspired to kill Jesus and those He described as *"My Sheep"* who followed Him.

The Pharisees saw and believed the Miracles Jesus did. They did not question the reality of the Miracles. They even tried to use His Miracles as *"evidence"* against Him (Mat. 12:9-14). Obviously, then, they *"believed"* in the Power of Jesus; at the same time, they were committed to killing Him.

His Disciples, on the other hand, whose *"belief"* in Him included a conscious commitment to *"follow"* Him, were promised Eternal Life. So, then, to be *"in Christ"* is not only *"believing"* but also *"following."*

What does it mean to *"follow"* Christ?

In II Thessalonians 3:6-9 the Apostle Paul admonished the faithful of the Church at Thessalonica to reject examples of those who behaved disorderly and to follow him. Did Paul mean that when he left town, they should form a caravan and troop after him wherever he went? Hardly. He plainly said that they should imitate his behavior. Therefore, *"following"* implies *"a conscious commitment to a course of action rather that a mere intellectual persuasion that something does indeed exist."*

Before leaving John, Chapter 10, let us look at one other important word that characterizes God's Sheep. Our *"unconditional eternal security"* brothers often use these Verses with the emphasis on Verses 28 and 29.

> *"And I give unto them Eternal Life; AND THEY SHALL NEVER PERISH, neither shall any man pluck them out of My Hand.*
> *"My Father, which gave them to Me, is greater than all; and no man is able to pluck them out of My Father's Hand"* (Jn. 10:28-29).

The phrase *"shall never perish"* has doubtless led many persons to ignore the significance of these two strong conditional words — *"hear"* and *"follow"* (Vs. 27) — which govern the promise of not perishing. We share in Christ's Life only as we *"hear"* and *"follow"* Him.

The word *"hear,"* like the word *"follow,"* is a present progressive verb, meaning . . .

> *"My sheep HEAR* [and keep on hearing] *My Voice . . . they FOLLOW* [and keep on following] *Me"* (Jn. 10:27).

Jesus also said that the Good Shepherd goes before His Sheep and leads them out, for they will not follow another shepherd, for His Sheep know only His Voice (Jn. 10:4, 14). Therefore, the phrase *"shall never perish"* (Vs. 28) is a conditional promise based on *"hearing"* and *"following."*

This same conditional promise is made elsewhere in John.

"Verily, verily, I say unto you, If a man KEEP My saying, he shall never see death" (Jn. 8:51).

"I am the Light of the world: he who FOLLOWS Me shall not walk in darkness, but shall have the Light of Life" (Jn. 8:12).

The promise of Eternal Life is indeed a blessed promise, but it is promised only for those who hear and follow.

We conclude, then, that within the Bible context the word *"believe"* means *"to commit oneself wholly to Jesus Christ as the Son of God, thereby taking on the Character and Personality of Christ, and dedicating one's life to be molded into His Image."* This, then, is the real meaning of the phrase *"in Christ"* as used in II Corinthians 5:17.

True Christians work to take upon themselves the nature, character, and spirit of the One in Whom they believe. They now strive with every ounce of energy to live for God to the highest degree of which they are capable. But someone may say, *"I thought we were Saved by Faith alone."* True. But as someone has clarified: *"It is Faith, alone, which saves; but the Faith that saves is not alone."*

The Apostle Paul wrote that the Grace of God that we receive through Faith teaches us . . .

"that, denying ungodliness and worldly lusts, WE SHOULD LIVE SOBERLY, RIGHTEOUSLY, AND GODLY, IN THIS PRESENT WORLD" (Titus 2:12).

A true conversion experience as opposed to a vocal one always includes a new attitude and a new commitment.

WORTHY TO ESCAPE

For those who are *"in Christ,"* Jesus issued a stern warning that they should be . . .

"ACCOUNTED WORTHY to escape all these things that shall come to pass [upon the world]" (Lk. 21:36).

The word *"worthy"* is so significant in the study and preparation for the Rapture that it would be remiss not to include it here even though the two terms, it seems, overlap.

"Watch you therefore, and pray always, that you may be ACCOUNTED WORTHY to escape all these things that

shall come to pass, and to stand before the Son of Man"
(Lk. 21:36).

The word *"worthy"* is a significant word as used in the New Testament; it means *"to have worth or value."* The Greek word for *"worthy"* is *axios*, meaning, *"deserving, to deem entirely deserving, fit."* Obviously, these definitions carry the idea of *"meritorious works."* Intrinsically, we are a people of infinite worth to God. He saw something in us that was worth redeeming; and thank God, He did redeem us through the atoning Work of Christ! Although Redemption is a free Gift of God, He intends to prove our worthiness by testing us so that we may see whether we are living and walking in the Faith; in other words, whether we are genuine. This is the reason Jesus exhorted us to . . .

"watch . . . and pray always"

. . . that we may be proved worthy to escape the wrath to come.

There is a vast difference between works for salvation and works that are a result of Salvation. The Apostle Paul explained this difference in the familiar Passage in Ephesians:

"For by Grace are you Saved through Faith; and that not of yourselves: it is the Gift of God:
"NOT OF WORKS, LEST ANY MAN SHOULD BOAST.
"For we are His workmanship, CREATED IN CHRIST JESUS UNTO GOOD WORKS, WHICH God has before ordained that WE SHOULD WALK IN THEM" (Eph. 2:8-10).

By Faith, all our *"good works"* are a product of our being *"in Christ"* and God working in our heart and life. It is proof that God is indeed working in our life. These good works were prepared *(ordained)* by God that we should walk in them.

Further on, the Apostle Paul said:

"For you were sometimes darkness, but now are you light in the Lord: WALK AS CHILDREN OF LIGHT . . . Proving what is acceptable unto the Lord" (Eph. 5:8-10).

"I therefore, the prisoner of the Lord, beseech you that you WALK WORTHY of the vocation wherewith you are called" (Eph. 4:1).

It is trials that prove our Faith, and proven Faith is . . .

"more precious than of gold that perishes" (I Pet. 1:7).

The Apostle Paul wrote to the Thessalonians concerning the worthiness of their Faith in relation to escaping the coming wrath.

"Wherefore also we pray always for you, that our God would COUNT YOU WORTHY OF THIS CALLING, and fulfil all the good pleasure of His goodness, and the work of Faith with power" (II Thess. 1:11).

No doubt, Paul's prayer and encouragement referred to the trials the Saints were already going through and commending them for their *"patience," "faith,"* and *"charity"* that they may be . . .

"COUNTED WORTHY of the Kingdom of God, for which you also suffer" (II Thess. 1:3-5).

Not only was this word *"worthy"* important to Paul, but it was used also throughout the Gospels. It was used first by John the Baptist in telling the Jews that were coming for the Baptism of Repentance that they should . . .

"Bring forth therefore fruits meet [WORTHY, axios] *for Repentance"* (Mat. 3:8)

The Greek scholar A.T. Robertson said of this Verse, *"John demands proof from these men of the New Life before he administers Baptism to them. 'The fruit is not the change of heart but the acts which result from it.'"*

The only proof that a man is *"in Christ"* is that his fruit will bear him out (Mat. 7:15-20; Jn. 15:1-8). If John demanded proof of their sincerity by the fruit that they produced, did Jesus do less? No! Notice how Jesus used the term to indicate those who are deserving to escape *"the wrath to come."*

"And into whatsoever city or town you shall enter, enquire who in it is WORTHY; and there abide till you go thence.
"And when you come into an house, salute it;
"And if the house be WORTHY, let your peace come upon it: but if it be not WORTHY, let your peace return to you" (Mat. 10:11-13).

And then the real test:

"He who loves father or mother more than Me is not WORTHY [not deserving] *of Me: and he who loves son or daughter more than Me is not WORTHY of Me.*

"And he who takes not his cross, and follows after Me, is not WORTHY of Me" (Mat. 10:37-38).

These are strong statements coming from the Lord Jesus and a far cry from the shallow, non-demanding preaching so prevalent in our pulpits today. Look back at the latter part of Matthew 10:10 for another quick reference:

"For the workman is WORTHY of his meat."

The opposite would be just as true: if he did not produce works, he would not be worthy of pay.

One other reference of this word, found in Christ's Parable of the Marriage Feast, may be mentioned here:

"Then said he to his servants, The wedding is ready, but they which were bidden were not WORTHY" (Mat. 22:8).

Here a rejection of the invitation is synonymous with unworthiness.

Yet a little further on in the Parable it is stated that not only those who refuse to come, but also those who accept the invitation but refuse to put on the wedding garment, are counted as unworthy (Mat. 22:11-14). The wedding garment, it seems, is a significant factor in proving a person's worthiness even though he has accepted the invitation. It is even more significant when we consider that the garment is a gift that will identify the guest.

This analogy of the garment is carried even further in the Lord's Message to the Church in Sardis:

"You have a few names even in Sardis which HAVE NOT DEFILED THEIR GARMENTS; and they shall walk with Me in white: for they are WORTHY" (Rev. 3:4).

Here it is not the rejection of the garment that proves a person's unworthiness, but, rather, the defiling of the garment. Those not defiling their garment . . .

"shall walk with Me in white: for they are WORTHY" (Vs. 4).

Why is this garment that is a gift to the Saints of such significance?

"And to her was granted that she should be arrayed in fine linen, clean and white: for the fine linen is the RIGHTEOUS-NESS of Saints" (Rev. 19:8).

Most translations read this as *"righteous deeds"* or *"righteous acts"* of the Saints. The scene is just prior to the Second Coming of Christ when the Marriage Supper of the Lamb takes place. The Bride is composed of all Saints of all ages who have put on the *"righteous acts"* of Christ, and are now dwelling in the New Jerusalem.

Again, is it any wonder that Jesus exhorted us to . . .

"Watch . . . and pray always, that you may be ACCOUNTED WORTHY to escape" (Lk. 21:36)

. . . that is, being found *"doing"* the Will of God? It may be worth mentioning here that one test of the New Birth is that a Christian . . .

"does Righteousness" (I Jn. 2:29).

Also, in John's day, just as today, many persons were being deceived by the easy-believing philosophy that *"it doesn't matter how you live, it's what you believe that counts."* Listen to John's warning for such a philosophy:

"Little children, let no man deceive you: HE WHO DOES RIGHTEOUSNESS IS RIGHTEOUS, even as He is Righteous.
"HE WHO COMMITS SIN IS OF THE DEVIL; for the Devil sins from the beginning. For this purpose the Son of God was manifested, that He might destroy the works of the Devil" (I Jn. 3:7-8).

EXAMINE YOURSELVES

The Apostle Paul told the Corinthians that . . .

"Every man's work shall be made manifest [tried]*"* (I Cor. 3:13).

He then expressed concern for his own labors among them:

"Are not you MY WORK IN THE LORD?" (I Cor. 9:1).

To be sure that his preaching and teaching were producing the necessary fruit to survive the trials ahead, he urged them:

> *"EXAMINE YOURSELVES, whether you be in the Faith; prove your own selves. Know you not your own selves, how that Jesus Christ is in you, except you be reprobates?"* (II Cor. 13:5).

The word *"examine"* here means *"to test, to try."* In other words, we should try ourselves to see whether Christ lives in our heart and life. It is not enough just to say, *"I believe"*; we must test ourselves continually.

The Apostle Paul mentioned to Titus that there are counterfeits to the Faith:

> *"THEY PROFESS THAT THEY KNOW GOD; BUT IN WORKS THEY DENY HIM, being abominable, and disobedient, and unto every good work reprobate"* (Titus 1:16).

The original meaning of the word *"reprobate"* is *"not to stand the test, to be disqualified, morally corrupt, unfit for any good deed"* (compare Rom. 1:28; II Tim. 3:8). *Works* and *words* must agree. Here the people professed that they knew God, but their life bore no fruit to prove their profession.

Because of the rejection of the preaching of . . .

> *"all the Counsel of God"* (Acts 20:27)

. . . there is a great emphasis on tolerance and permissiveness on the part of the religious world. Too, because of the humanistic influence on the Church and society — teaching that man is basically good, and all that society needs is education and freedom from the Judeo-Christian restraints that have hindered man's progress — there has been a de-emphasizing of the *"judgment"* teaching of the Bible. A Preacher today who reasons with his congregation over such things as . . .

> *"righteousness, temperance, and judgment to come"* (Acts 24:25)

. . . as Paul reasoned with Felix and Drusilla, would not last long in a modern pulpit.

Today it is considered negative thinking to talk about sin and *"judgment to come."* But is it negative to insist on the same demands as Jesus and Paul insisted? Listen to the demand of Jesus:

31

"He who finds his life shall lose it: and he who loses his life for My sake shall find it" (Mat. 10:39).

Jesus was talking not about *"works salvation,"* but about the fact that those who desired to follow him must obey Him. Why? For their own good. Only as we submit to His Way are we able to be WORTHY. Left to ourselves, we would fail.

PETER'S USE

The Apostle Peter summed up this argument of testing oneself in language too plain to be misunderstood:

"Whereby are given unto us exceeding great and Precious Promises: that by these you might be partakers of the Divine Nature, having escaped the corruption that is in the world through lust.

"And beside this, GIVING ALL DILIGENCE, ADD TO YOUR FAITH VIRTUE; AND TO VIRTUE KNOWLEDGE;

"AND TO KNOWLEDGE TEMPERANCE; AND TO TEMPERANCE PATIENCE; AND TO PATIENCE GODLINESS;

"AND TO GODLINESS BROTHERLY KINDNESS; AND TO BROTHERLY KINDNESS CHARITY.

"For if these things be in you, and abound, they make you that you shall neither be barren nor unfruitful in the knowledge of our Lord Jesus Christ.

"But he who lacks these things is blind, and cannot see afar off, and has forgotten that he was purged from his old sins.

"Wherefore the rather, Brethren, GIVE DILIGENCE TO MAKE YOUR CALLING AND ELECTION SURE: FOR IF YOU DO THESE THINGS, YOU SHALL NEVER FALL:

"For so an entrance shall be Ministered unto you abundantly into the Everlasting Kingdom of our Lord and Saviour Jesus Christ" (II Pet. 1:4-11).

The Apostle Peter agreed with Jesus Christ, the Apostle John, and the Apostle Paul on the necessary fruit as proof of a genuine Christian experience. Surely we ought to do as Peter exhorted:

"Give diligence to make your calling and election sure: for if you do these things, you shall never fall."

If there were no possibility of falling or proving ourselves unworthy, this warning would never have been issued.

Is it any wonder, then, that Jesus exhorted us — yea, warned us — to . . .

> *"Watch . . . and pray . . . that you may be ACCOUNTED WORTHY to escape all these things that shall come to pass, and to stand before the Son of Man"* (Lk. 21:36)?

Beloved, what is your reaction to the trials of this life that come your way? This is God's way of testing your Faith, that it may be tried in the fires of adversity so that the true gold will come forth and the dross burned off so that you may be *"accounted worthy."*

FOUR CONDITIONS FOR REMAINING IN CHRIST

Once again, if it were impossible for Christians to be caught in the condition of unsuitability to meet the Lord, there would be no reason for Paul's exhorting Christians to avoid falling into this condition. Let us, then, preface this study by categorically stating that we do not believe that everyone who professes to be a Christian will be included in the Rapture.

A shocking statement?

Perhaps. But a careful study of the Word of God will verify this position. We will clarify this position by studying four Scriptural conditions that will qualify a person for the Rapture: (1) sleeplessness, (2) watchfulness, (3) soberness, and (4) coveredness.

SLEEPLESSNESS

Sometime after the rise of Adolf Hitler to power in Germany, many Germans perceived the real intent of Hitler that was hidden behind his rhetoric to put a Volkswagen in every German carport. After organizing a door-to-door campaign to warn the German people of what lay ahead, they were met by a complacent, self-satisfied public that slammed the door on them for disturbing their peace.

It is with this in mind that we study the Apostle Paul's warning to the Thessalonians that professing Christians, who are asleep spiritually, are living in danger of missing the Rapture.

The Greek word that the Apostle Paul used for *"sleep"* (I Thess. 5:6) is the Greek word *katheudo,* and means *"to repose oneself in sleep."* The same Greek word is used in Matthew 25:5 to describe the faithless, careless, indifferent virgins.

However, context determines the Biblical meaning that the Holy Spirit intends. In I Thessalonians 5:6, therefore, *katheudo* is used metaphorically as *"carnal insensibility to Divine things involving conformity to the world."* The Apostle Paul contrasted spiritual sleep (Vs. 6) with the natural sleep that comes at night and with the drunkenness that dulls a person's senses (Vs. 7).

Another Greek word for *"sleep"* may be mentioned here that carries the same connotation as *katheudo,* but with a little different slant. This word is found in Romans 13:11.

"And that, knowing the time, and now it is high time to AWAKE out of SLEEP: for now is our Salvation nearer than when we believed.

"The night is far spent, the day is at hand: let us therefore cast off the works of darkness, and let us put on the armour of light.

"Let us walk honestly, as in the day; not in rioting and drunkenness, not in chambering and wantonness, not in strife and envying.

"But put you on the Lord Jesus Christ, and make not provision for the flesh, to fulfil the lusts thereof" (Rom. 13:11-14).

The Greek word for *"sleep"* that we are exhorted to *"awake out of"* is *hypnou,* from the root word *hypnos.* It is the same word from which our word *"hypnosis"* is derived. *"Hypnosis"* is a *"state that resembles sleep, but is induced by a person whose suggestions are readily accepted by the subject."*

Think of that! What better definition could we have of Spiritual Sleep than that of listening to the voice of the Devil (induced by a person) who suggests that we turn our eyes from the Lord and toward those things that direct our attention to the world?

Paul's warning in the light of the imminent Return of the Lord Jesus Christ is to awake us out of our Spiritual Conformity to the world and to *"put on Christ"*; that is, our sole interest in life must be the same as that of our Lord to enter into His Views, His Thinking, and to imitate Him in all things. Why? Because, as the Apostle Peter said:

"Be sober, be vigilant; because your adversary the Devil, as a roaring lion, walks about, seeking whom he may devour" (I Pet. 5:8).

No sooner had the Children of God come out of Egyptian bondage than they became disenchanted and disillusioned and began to turn back to the beggarly elements of the world. The Christian experience is similar. When people are first Saved and begin their Christian walk, they are usually on a mountaintop high. For a time they continue bouncing from mountaintop to mountaintop, or, as King Solomon described it . . .

> *"leaping upon the mountains, skipping upon the hills"* (Song of Sol. 2:8).

But sooner or later the season wears on. The petals fall in the rose garden until the thorns begin to show. The cherry bowl begins to display more pits than cherries. . . .

Unfortunately, most Christians believe their Christian gardens will never become invaded by weeds. They are taught by overzealous teachers and misguided preachers that a Christian's walk should never come down from the mountaintops, but it always does. Why? Because it is only during these periods that we are able to stand back, evaluate our Christian Growth, and recognize the areas where we need more work.

Faith that has never been tested is a Faith that can never be quite certain. That is the reason that our reactions during these periods of *"valley"* Christianity determine the outcome of our Christian walk. Every moon walk has its reentry, and every spiritual high has its return to Earth. A solid enduring relationship with God is something to be arrived at only with hard work, sweat, and tears.

Too many Christians become indifferent with the passage of time. Living for Christ, in Christ, and like Christ becomes a bore. Attending church can become an inconvenience. If we fail to work at it and fail continually to renew our commitment and review our Blessings, it is possible for us to fall by the wayside.

It is always more fun to talk about the Blessings and the highs and the glory and the grandeur. But a farm would soon fall into disrepair and ruin if the chores were not done every day. If the cows were not milked twice a day, they would soon stop giving milk. If they were not fed daily and their stalls cleaned, they would soon sicken and die.

Chores keep the world turning. And if we neglect our Spiritual Chores, our eternal farm is going to wreck and ruin. We should spend more time on the chores of our Spiritual Walk rather than spending so much time lifting our eyes to the glories above.

We like to gather a crowd on a hill and point out the absolute beauty of the well-tended farm spread out below us. But, unfortunately, we do not give equal time to the cultivation that produced those tended fields.

A Christian has to make a conscious decision to walk in the Ways of

God. Our human, carnal nature is such that we crave constant stimulation. We are easily drawn off into the world. But excitement and stimulation can come from the enemy. A Christian who wishes to be truly *"in Christ"* — to be an overcomer — must decide first whether he is willing to dedicate himself to this and every waking moment of his life.

We must constantly decide we are going to do these things necessary to grow as Christians — things that require energy and effort. Jesus said:

"He who is faithful in that which is least is faithful also in much" (Lk. 16:10).

These daily chores are the basis of the Christian life. Let us never lose sight of one fact: we do not do these things to earn Salvation or to win favor with God. No one earns anything from God. Everything we have from God comes to us by Grace. We are the ones who need the maturity that is the outgrowth of a daily consistent Christian walk. God can get along with or without our *"works"*; we cannot.

Just as a dedicated farmer does not fall asleep as he rushes from one chore to another, the Christian who spends each day exercising his Spiritual Gifts is neither blind nor prey to Satan's devices. The problem comes when the Christian decides to take a break. He becomes bored, takes a few days off to refresh himself with an excursion into the world. Then, he becomes vulnerable to Satan's serene song and soon falls prey to his hypnotic lures.

How many times have you been present among gatherings of *"Christians,"* where you mentioned revival, and no one perked up? You tried to get a conversation going about some Bible Passage, and then someone brought up the Super Bowl or the latest movie. What happened? Everyone was suddenly interested. These are Christians who are asleep in Christ and awake to the things of the world.

What elicits responses in your own heart? What excites you? What gets you out of your chair and heading for some activity?

The true answer may come as a shock to you. It is almost as though the world has taken a spiritual sedative. We are asleep at the wheel. Church services are a bore. Living for God has become a bore. God's Word just is not as exciting as it used to be.

Or is it? Are we the ones who are out of step? A great percentage of the Christian segment of the world's population has been lulled to sleep by Satan's hypnotic lures. We believe when the Holy Spirit gave the words to the Apostle Paul, He was putting them there for Christians in this day as well.

Wake up, Christian world! Sleeping Christians are not going to have an alarm clock just before the Rapture.

WATCHFULNESS

The second condition that will result in the Christian's worthiness to be included in the Rapture is that of watchfulness. The Apostle Paul said:

"Let us WATCH" (I Thess. 5:6).

There are four words used in the New Testament for *"watch"* that are used in relation to Christ's return. Incidentally, these four words are used also in Passages dealing with moral and ethical conduct.

Two of these words — *gregoreo* and *agrupneo* — mean *"to be on the alert, to be wide awake spiritually."* The force of these words is to point up the urgency of the situation.

If we do not set an eternal vigilance on the Return of Christ, we are in danger of missing out. The Apostle Peter's thinking went along the same lines as the Apostle Paul's when he warned:

"Be sober, be VIGILANT [gregoreo]*; because your adversary the Devil, as a roaring lion, walks about, seeking whom he may devour"* (I Pet. 5:8).

Let us turn to the Gospel of Mark to illustrate the use of these two most significant words of warning to the Christians concerning watchfulness.

"But of that day and that hour knows no man, no, not the Angels which are in Heaven, neither the Son, but the Father.
"TAKE YOU HEED, WATCH AND PRAY: FOR YOU KNOW NOT WHEN THE TIME IS.
"For the Son of Man is as a man taking a far journey, Who left His House, and gave authority to His Servants, and to every man his work, and commanded the porter to WATCH.
"WATCH you therefore: for you know not when the Master of the house comes, at evening, or at midnight, or at the cockcrowing, or in the morning:
"LEST COMING SUDDENLY HE FIND YOU SLEEPING.
"And what I say unto you I say unto all, WATCH" (Mk. 13:32-37).

This Parable illustrates the necessity of watchfulness. The word *"watch"* is used in this Parable four times. Let us look at each use of this word *"watch."*

In Verse 33 Jesus said:

> *"Take you heed, WATCH."*

The word here means *"to chase sleep, to be sleepless,"* and expresses not mere wakefulness but a watchfulness of those who are intent upon doing anything.

In Verse 34 He commanded the porter to watch. The word here is sometimes translated *"vigilant alertness,"* not as the same word in Verse 33.

Verse 35 begins with *"watch"* and again the urgency of watching is emphasized.

> *"You know not when the Master of the house comes"*

. . . so be watching. Again, the warning in Verse 36:

> *"Lest coming suddenly He find you sleeping."*

In Verse 37 the last use of the word is capitalized emphasizing the force of the word — the urgency of the hour.

> *"For the Son of Man is as a man taking a far journey, Who left His House"* (Vs. 34)

. . . and does not say when He will return. But He said, considering the urgency of it:

> *"What I say unto you I say unto all, WATCH."*

When a person is going on a long-sought-after vacation, he usually spends a restless, uncomfortable night in anticipation of the upcoming departure. For the true Christian it is hard to rest comfortably in the world when he is anticipating something so much better.

We have often seen the picture of the restless, sleepless mother and father, looking down the trail waiting for the long-lost prodigal to return.

The helmsman of a ship fights back sleep to maintain his bearing, knowing that the mightiest wave will slide under the heel if the prow of the ship meets it head-on. Our Captain says, *"Take heed, be watchful,"* just as a sea captain says, *"Mind your helm."*

Notice again in the Parable that the Son of Man . . .

"commanded the porter to WATCH" (Vs. 34).

Here, as in Verse 35, the Apostles are compared to doorkeepers (porters); as the captain of the guard made his rounds at night through the Temple, the guards were to rise and salute him. Any guard found asleep on duty was beaten or his garments set on fire.

It is self-evident that under that severe penalty not many guards would drowse off to sleep. This use of the word was mentioned again by Jesus as He spoke to the Apostle John:

"Behold, I come as a thief. Blessed is he who WATCHES, and KEEPS HIS GARMENTS, lest he walk naked, and they see his shame" (Rev.16:15).

What a warning! What an incentive to alertness!

One lexicon says that the word *gregoreo* comes from a root word meaning *"collecting our faculties."* In the light of the soon Return of the Lord Jesus Christ, we should be *"collecting our faculties,"* lest we lose our garments and *"walk naked"* and ashamed.

The Christian who drowses away at his Christianity is imperiling his Salvation. All too many Christians count on God to keep them alert. They feel it is God's duty to warn them as each new wave approaches. Unfortunately, it is not the duty of the captain of the ship to stand the wheel watch; it is the person at the helm who must maintain constant vigilance if he is to see the voyage to a successful conclusion. The helmsman who falls asleep and endangers the ship is eligible for grave and disciplinary action. Christians who fail to maintain their vigilance can expect no better. There are consequences for our every action. Spiritual consequences are no less real than worldly ones.

This is the reason the Apostle Paul said:

"I die daily" (I Cor. 15:31).

The great Apostle of Christ brought his body . . .

"into subjection"

. . . every waking day . . .

"lest that by any means, when I have preached to others, I

myself should be a castaway" (I Cor. 9:27).

And if such a magnificent man of God found it necessary to remain ever vigilant (lest he fall by the wayside), who are we to become overconfident?

Yet Christians are becoming smug. Christian attention is wandering. Clergy and laity are becoming immersed in this world. It is a new day in which we live. The old Scriptures no longer count. Practices that would have been denounced a short time ago are accepted now. Everyone is doing it. It is a new day. . . .

But is it?

King Solomon wrote:

> *"There is no new thing under the sun"* (Eccl. 1:9).

Satan knows there is nothing new under the sun. The modern morals and the new permissiveness are nothing new to him. He has promoted the same things in Greece, in Rome, in Sodom and Gomorrah, and in Babylon.

> *"Is there any thing whereof it may be said, See, this is new? it has been already of old time, which was before us"* (Eccl. 1:10).

The new morality is new to us only because we were not alive in ancient days to see the old morality. And if we fall for the new morality now, the same consequences that befell Greece, Rome, Sodom and Gomorrah, and Babylon will befall our civilization.

Satan is breaking through the doors of our once moral and Spiritual Strongholds. Today he is bombarding our mind through pornographic movies which come right into our living rooms, billboards, magazines, indecent dress, public scenes that once would have caused people to blush. Many Christians sit through these movies, laugh at the openly obscene jokes, and then wonder why their relationship with God is not what it used to be.

These Christians have been lulled to sleep. They have been put under a hypnotic trance by Satan because they have not watched. They do not WATCH what they see, where they go, and what they say — and all of this despite the fact that the Holy Spirit has enjoined them to WATCH. Not to watch and pray is to prove oneself unworthy to be included in the Rapture.

SOBERNESS

The Greek word for *"sober" (nepho)* signifies to be free from the influence of intoxicants; it does not in itself imply watchfulness, but is used in association with it.

The antonym for *"sobriety"* is *"drunkenness."* Drunkenness involves the deadening of one's senses. A person's faculties of reasoning are dulled, rendering him incapable of making serious decisions of judgments. Proverbs says to . . .

> *"Give strong drink unto him who is ready to perish"* (Prov. 31:6)

. . . for it will deaden his senses and render him insensible to pain. It was a custom to offer strong drink to condemned criminals to relieve their suffering. It was offered to our Lord Jesus Christ, but He refused (Mat. 27:34; Ps. 69:21). He chose rather to enter into His Suffering sober-minded. The work He was doing for man was too serious to face with anything less than a sound mind.

Just as the Apostle Paul used the word *"drunkenness"* to imply darkness, he used the word *"soberness"* to imply walking in the Light. Drunkenness is characterized by revelry, frivolity, and levity. Spiritual matters should not be a source of levity. The Christian is to be serious-minded in light of the soon Return of the Lord in Glory. In view of His soon Coming the Apostle Peter exhorted:

> *"But the end of all things is at hand: be you therefore SOBER, and WATCH unto prayer"* (I Pet. 4:7).

In other words, God intends us to act and speak with sobriety instead of foolishness that characterizes a drunkard. The Apostle Paul spoke of levity as a form of foolishness:

> *"Neither filthiness, NOR FOOLISH TALKING, NOR JESTING, WHICH ARE NOT CONVENIENT: but rather giving of thanks"* (Eph. 5:4).

Anyone taking the things of God lightly is not facing facts as they are presented to God. On the other hand, Satan does not look on his campaign as a source of mirth and amusement. He is deadly serious about accomplishing his ends.

Tom Landry, the coach of the Dallas Cowboys football team, once fired a linebacker because he was clowning on the sidelines when the Cowboys were being badly beaten. Certainly a football game is no great consequence in God's Plan for the ages, but Coach Landry's attitude demonstrates something about Christian commitment. His attitude toward commitment and dedication, sobriety, and facing a challenge exactly parallels the point the Holy Spirit of God made in II Thessalonians.

A team going into a game with a lackadaisical attitude is more likely to lose than a team with a tight-lipped serious determination to win! Sober resolution is a factor that cannot be weighed in the balance against ability, coordination, or statistics. The team soberly dedicated to taking home the victory overcomes the statistical reasons why they cannot win.

In approaching the Cross, Jesus expressed:

> *"Therefore HAVE I SET MY FACE LIKE A FLINT, and I know that I shall not be ashamed"* (Isa. 50:7).

We are not promoting long faces by any means. We are denouncing the hail-fellow-well-met, eat-drink-and-be-merry attitude. This spells involvement with the world. A smile should be the badge of the Saved Christian. Who has more reason to smile? But a smile does not necessarily mean a lighthearted approach to a task. Consecration is an inward thing.

We are to face our godly duties and responsibilities as men and not as immature children. The Apostle Paul said:

> *"Be alert and on your guard; stand firm in your faith* (that is, in your conviction respecting man's relationship to God and Divine things, keeping the trust and holy fervor born of faith and a part of it). *Act like men and be courageous; grow in strength"* (I Cor. 16:13, Amplified).

To be alert and on your guard, along with acting like men, will result in sober thinking. Knowing the foolishness and immaturity of the youth, the Apostle Paul counseled Titus:

> *"Young men likewise exhort to be SOBER MINDED.*
> *"In all things showing yourself A PATTERN OF GOOD WORKS: in Doctrine showing UNCORRUPTNESS, GRAVITY, SINCERITY,*
> *"SOUND SPEECH, that cannot be condemned; that he who is of the contrary part may be ashamed, having no evil thing to say of you"* (Titus 2:6-8).

It is this sober approach to the world of which the Apostle John spoke:

> *"Love not the world, neither the things that are in the world. If any man love the world, the love of the Father is not in him.*

"For all that is in the world, the lust of the flesh, and the lust of the eyes, and the pride of life, is not of the Father, but is of the world.

"And the world passes away, and the lust thereof: but he who does the Will of God abides forever" (I Jn. 2:15-17).

Victory is assured, John said, by doing the Will of God.

Although we are in this world, our views should be always toward higher things. Our only concern should lie in growing ever closer to God. We should be developing in the Lord. Christian golfers spend hours smoothing out their swings. How many are willing to devote as much time to smoothing out their Spiritual Attitudes and growing maturely?

Anything worth doing is worth practicing. Practice involves long hours devoted to perfecting our areas of interest. Is anything more important in life than seeing God's great Plan brought to completion? What, then, is more important than practicing and perfecting our maturity as Christians? The Apostle Paul summed it up:

"Brethren, I count not myself to have apprehended: but this one thing I do, forgetting those things which are behind, and reaching forth unto those things which are before,

"I PRESS TOWARD THE MARK FOR THE PRIZE OF THE HIGH CALLING OF GOD IN CHRIST JESUS" (Phil. 3:13-14).

Praise God, what an exhortation! Christian perfection is practicing and striving onward toward our high calling in Christ Jesus . . .

"unto a perfect man, unto the measure of the stature of the fullness of Christ" (Eph. 4:13).

Those persons enmeshed in the world may find their eyes averted at the moment the Lord Jesus beckons. Lot's wife looked back after she had been saved, and a pillar of salt is her only memorial (Gen. 19:26; Lk. 17:32). Christians, too, involved in the world should take warning from her experience. Those who fail to continue watching soberly could end up as tragically as Lot's wife.

The Rapture could take place at any moment. Let us be sober-minded, watching and praying always that we be *"accounted worthy."*

COVEREDNESS

The last condition of which Paul spoke in I Thess. 5:1-11, as a condition for worthiness to escape the wrath to come, is that of a state of coveredness.

"Let us, who are of the day, be sober, PUTTING ON the breastplate of Faith and Love; and for an helmet, the Hope of Salvation" (I Thess. 5:8).

Many Scripture Passages exhort us to put on something. Paul, in speaking to the Galatians, stated that we are to put on Christ (Gal. 3:27), meaning that we have been clothed with Christ; we are to assume His Person and Character. In Ephesians 4:22-24 Paul said that we are to put off the old man and that we are to put on the new man, again meaning we are to be clothed with Christ. Ephesians 6:11 explains it a little more fully. We are told to put on the whole Armour of God.

In other words, the Scripture directs us to be completely covered by God. Think of the import of that!

Notice that Scripture uses, by choice, a military metaphor to prescribe our posture as Christians. Why? Because we are engaged in war. Many Christians tend to minimize this or forget it altogether. To them the Christian walk is a side dish on the banqueting table of life. In actuality, our continuing war with Satan should be the centerpiece of all our waking activities.

This is the war to the death! Scripture tells us of the wages of sin — death (Rom. 6:23). The whole goal of Satan's battle in the Earth is to impose death (through sin) on as many souls as possible. He has his sights trained on the soul of every living person. Satan's only aim in life is . . .

"to steal, and to kill, and to destroy" (Jn. 10:10).

The moment we drop our guard, weaken our defenses, and relax our vigilance (in short, fail to remain sober) we become likely candidates for defeat by Satan.

There is no one in the world more subtle than Satan. We are warned of this in Scripture (Gen. 3:1). *"Subtlety"* implies *"underhandedness, deceit, and treachery."* Satan does not defeat enemies by storming strongholds. He gains victory by tunneling away at the unsuspected weak spot in the wall. This is the reason the Apostle Paul exhorted:

"PUT ON THE WHOLE ARMOUR OF GOD, that you may be able to stand against the wiles of the Devil" (Eph. 6:11).

In Ephesians 6:11-17 Paul elaborated on this armour with which we are to be clothed. This is the same armour that clothed Jesus in His earthly Walk. When we put on Him, we are putting on the armour that He provided. Unlike the armour of King Saul that would not fit the lad David (I Sam. 17:38-39), Jesus' Armour fits all sizes.

Let us look at this armour that we are to *"put on."* Notice that WE are to put it on.

> *"Wherefore take unto YOU THE WHOLE ARMOUR OF GOD, that YOU may be able to withstand in the evil day, and having done all, to stand.*
>
> *"Stand therefore, having your LOINS GIRD ABOUT WITH TRUTH, and having* (done all, to stand. Stand therefore, having your LOINS GIRD ABOUT WITH TRUTH, and having) *on the BREASTPLATE OF RIGHTEOUSNESS;*
>
> *"And your FEET SHOD WITH THE PREPARATION OF THE GOSPEL OF PEACE;*
>
> *"Above all, taking the SHIELD OF FAITH, wherewith you shall be able to quench all the fiery darts of the wicked.*
>
> *"And take the HELMET OF SALVATION, and the SWORD OF THE SPIRIT, which is the Word of God"* (Eph. 6:13-17).

"Take unto you the whole Armour of God" means to *"put on the whole Armour of God,"* as the Apostle Paul stated (compare I Thess. 5:8). It is something that we are to do. Too many Christians are resting on their past experience, that supposedly gave them an eternal ticket to Heaven while their life has been characterized by such defeat and frustration, that it makes a person wonder if there is any Power in the Blood of Christ. The Blood truly is Power-producing, but it must be *applied* just as the Armour of God has to be *put on* to become effective.

Notice the various parts of the armour that are to be put on.

BELT OF TRUTH (Eph. 6:14). We are able to stand . . .

> *"having tightened the BELT OF TRUTH around your loins"* (Eph. 6:14, *Amplified*).

The loins are described as the seat of power. *"To strike through the loins"* is to strike a fatal blow. The girdle formed the hinge, or the bond, that united the many pieces of armour. Truth, the Apostle Paul said, is the hinge that gives character and unity to the armour.

> *"[God] desires truth in the inward parts"* (Ps. 51:6).

As long as we hold back or fail to operate in all the Truth, we are vulnerable to Satan's attacks. Truth always means *"reality."* Satan can spot a phony or an insincere person a mile away. Jesus said that He was the Truth (Jn. 14:6); and every Word that He spoke and the Life that He lived verified the reality of that statement. Jesus spoke only the things that God told Him to speak; He did only the things God told Him to do. He stated that He had given us His Word and that His Word is Truth (Jn. 17:17). Therefore, by keeping His Word, we can abide in His Truth and His Truth will make us free (Jn. 8:32).

Biblical Truth is absolute. It is not relative or depending on the situation. The Christian has been liberated from having to cover up through little *"white"* lies to justify his actions. The Christian no longer has anything to hide; his life is an open book. He no longer has anything to fear. If he makes a costly mistake on his job, he need not cover up through deceit or half-truths to justify himself, to save his job. He is free to tell the truth regardless of the outcome. He knows that God honors truth in the inward parts, and rewards those who . . .

"worship Him in spirit and in truth" (Jn. 4:24).

One connotation of truth is that it is *"reality."* To abide in truth is to be a real person, transparent. We can be honest about our limitations, fears, and inferiorities. Our only purpose in life is to please God.

Jesus told the woman at the well that she had had five husbands. (The story is told in Jn. 4:4-42.) This awakened her to the reality of the lie that she had been living. A radical change took place in her life. She became transparent and no longer had to hide. She returned to her city and shared openly that she had met a man that had revealed to her the reality of the life she was living. Jesus said:

"HE WHO DOES TRUTH COMES TO THE LIGHT, THAT HIS DEEDS MAY BE MADE MANIFEST" (Jn. 3:21).

This truth, however, does not come only through a head knowledge of Jesus, but also is derived by doing God's Will.

"IF ANY MAN WILL DO HIS WILL, HE SHALL KNOW of the Doctrine, whether it be of God, or whether I speak of Myself" (Jn. 7:17).

One translation reads:

"If any man wills to do the Will of God."

The word *"will"* means to *"desire"* above everything to do and live according to God's Word. This desire comes from deep inside a man. We must *will* to do it. Although emotional experiences are good and beautiful, these in themselves will not lead a person to the truth. Truth is known only when there is a willingness *"to do the Will of God."*

Jesus emphasized this truth by stating:

> *"True worshippers shall worship the Father in spirit and in truth"* (Jn. 4:23).

To worship God in truth is to worship Him by living a life of reality according to His Word. Jesus said:

> *"He who is of God hears God's Words"* (Jn. 8:47).

The belt of Truth, then, is the power hinge that unites all the rest of the armour.

BREASTPLATE OF RIGHTEOUSNESS (Eph. 6:14). The second part of the armour is the breastplate. In I Thessalonians 5:8 the breastplate is described as *"faith and love."* The stiff Roman breastplate caused a soldier to *"stand upright."* The spiritual application of Righteousness is *"moral rectitude"* or moral and spiritual uprightness. The implication, then, is that we are to live in a right relationship with both God and man. Our life is to be viewed as upright before God and man.

The breastplate covered the vital organs and those that were more vulnerable. When the breastplate is made of *"faith and love,"* nothing can penetrate it. Without *"faith and love"* we are nothing more than clanging armour and are unable to please God (I Cor. 13:1, Heb. 11:6). We are to stand *"foursquare"* with our neighbor and upright before God in *"faith and love."* No Devil's dart can penetrate *"faith and love."*

SHOES OF THE GOSPEL (Eph. 6:15). The next part of the armour covers the feet. We are to be . . .

> *"shod with the preparation of the Gospel of Peace"* (Eph. 6:15).

This means that the Believer is to have a sure footing, a firm foundation that will enable him to walk worthy of his calling. The word denotes *"preparation that will result in a harmonious relationship between God and man, and man with man."*

When a person knows that he has been reconciled to God through Christ and, as best as he understands, is walking in Truth and Love according to the Word of God (Eph. 4:15), then and only then does he have the . . .

"Peace of God, which passes all understanding" (Phil. 4:7).

The feet symbolize walking:

"Walk in Newness of Life" (Rom. 6:4) . . .

"Walk worthy of the vocation wherewith you are called" (Eph. 4:1) . . .

"Walk circumspectly, not as fools, but as wise" (Eph. 5:15) . . .

"Walk worthy of the Lord unto all pleasing, being fruitful in every good work" (Col. 1:10) . . .

"Walk honestly toward them who are without" (I Thess. 4:12) . . .

"Walk in the Light, as He is in the Light" (I Jn. 1:7) . . . *et al.*

No man can have the peace of God as long as he is not walking the straight and narrow path. Every man knows when his walk is out of conformity with the Will of God. As a result, his life is characterized by confusion and condemnation. However, when he makes Peace with God and begins to walk in the narrow path, the Spirit will bear witness with his spirit that he is a Child of God (Rom. 8:14, 16).

SHIELD OF FAITH (Eph. 6:16). The shield was a piece of armour shaped like a door that the soldier held out in front of him to ward off the arrows of the enemy. The shield of Faith is the Word of God that enables a person to ward off the darts of evil thoughts, lusts, passions, and temptations of various kinds. Faith is the opposite of fear, which brings torment (I Jn. 4:18). Faith is the confidence we have in Christ (I Jn. 3:21; 5:14) that the darts of the enemy cannot penetrate.

The old shields were made of wood, and the enemy shot fiery darts that would ignite the wood, thus burning away their protection. Our shield of Faith is covered with precious metals from the nuggets of God's Word that are impenetrable as long as we hold our shield high. Praise God!

It is said that Abraham . . .

"staggered not at the Promise of God through unbelief; but was strong in Faith, giving Glory to God;
"And being fully persuaded that, what He had promised, He was able also to perform" (Rom. 4:20-21).

When we stagger not at God's Promises, written in His Word, just as Abraham, we put to flight the Devil and all of his fiery darts. We are Justified by Faith (Rom. 3:28); we are Sanctified by Faith (Rom. 3:22; Phil. 3:9); we are Glorified by Faith (Rom. 8:30).

> *"We have access by Faith into this Grace wherein we stand, and rejoice in Hope of the Glory of God"* (Rom. 5:2).

Therefore, the shield of Faith is to be our banner. Let us lift high the banner.

When we put on our shield of Faith and tie it firmly in place with the lacing of love, it hardly weighs an ounce; but it will protect us from the ugly, most fearsome piece of shrapnel Satan can throw our way. Without that Shield we have no Hope of escape and are accounted *un*worthy to escape *"the wrath to come."*

HELMET OF SALVATION (Eph. 6:17). The helmet of Salvation is described in I Thessalonians 5:8 as the *"Hope of Salvation."* This means that our awareness of the final outcome of this battle protects us against any propaganda from the enemy. We know which is the winning side. It is much easier to get through the hard times when we are assured of a seat in the convertible during the ticker-tape parade. This is what God means in this Scripture. Our head (mind) is protected by the *"Blessed Hope"* (assurance) that ultimately we win.

The Apostle Paul said that we are *"Saved by Hope"* (Rom. 8:24), but someone may say, *"I thought we were Saved by Faith."* We are. The word *"hope"* means *"a favorable and confident expectation."* It has to do with the unseen and the future, whereas Faith has to do with the past and the present. Faith claims Salvation now as a present experience based on a past event. Hope says, *"I have it, but I have not yet entered into the fullness of the resurrected life that is still future."*

The appearing of Jesus in the air is future and is referred to as the *"Blessed Hope"* (Titus 2:13). Again, the Apostle Paul spoke of the . . .

> *"Hope and Resurrection of the dead"* (Acts 23:6).

The Rapture of the Believer is . . .

> *"the Hope of Salvation"* (I Thess. 5:8) . . .

> *"Hope of Eternal Life"* (Titus 1:2; 3:7)

. . .that is, the full manifestation and realization of that Life which is already a Believer's possession. To this could be added . . .

"good Hope" (II Thess. 2:16) . . .

"a lively Hope" (I Pet. 1:3) . . .

"a better Hope" (Heb. 7:19) . . . *et al.*

The *"Hope of Salvation,"* as used in I Thessalonians 5:8, means that Salvation is not an unforfeitable possession until the resurrected Life begins. There is a danger of forfeiting our Salvation unless we are equipped with the whole Armour of God. A soldier who refuses to wear his battle array will not last long in the heat of the conflict. Likewise, a Christian who refuses to prepare himself with God's Armour will not stand long in battle.

SWORD OF THE SPIRIT (Eph. 6:17). This is the only offensive weapon that the Soldier of God is to carry into battle; that is,

"the Sword of the Spirit, which is the Word of God."

The word used here for *"Word"* is the Greek *rhema,* meaning *"the spoken Word of God."* The Sword, the Word of God, when quoted in times of trials and temptations, will cut in pieces the snare of the enemy. We are not to stand back nonchalantly, resting in the fact that we have the helmet of Salvation and the breastplate of Righteousness and our feet shod with the preparation of the Gospel of Peace, but we are also to enter into the thick of the battle, carrying the Sword, the Word of God.

The complacent Christian who says he never has any problems is the Christian who never enters into the thick of the battle. The ones who enter into the heat of the conflict are those who are going to have the scars. They are the ones who are going to have the bruises; they are going to have the hurts; but they are going to deal the Devil a tremendous blow if they know how to rightly divide the Word of Truth (II Tim. 2:15) and to wield their Sword effectively.

The writer of the Book of Hebrews says that if we are going to enter into the Rest (Heb. 4:11), that full Victory, that full Assurance, and not fall, we must use the Word of God.

"The Word of God is quick, and powerful, and sharper than any two-edged sword, piercing even to the dividing asunder of soul and spirit, and of the joints and marrow, and is a discerner of the thoughts and intents of the heart" (Heb. 4:12).

In other words, the Word of God is powerful just like a two-edged sword. When we enter into trials or temptations, conflicts, and the onslaught of the devil, and we raise up our banner, our sword, and begin to quote the Word of God, the Devil has to flee. He cannot stand against the Word of God — it cuts, it hurts, it divides body, soul, and spirit, and reveals to a man the inner thoughts and intents of his heart.

Most people will testify that under powerful anointed preaching the Word of God pierced their soul, brought conviction, and restlessness until they made their way to the altar, and there had that sword removed, and then . . .

"The Peace of God, which passes all understanding" (Phil. 4:7)

. . . flooded their heart and their soul. This is the Sword of the Spirit, the spoken Word of God.

Time is so short. The Trump of God will sound soon. Only if we use this time in preparing ourselves for that Great Day can we be assured of participating in the Rapture. Slothful Christians are treading on quivering sand. Prudent Christians will turn their eyes away from the world and toward the Word. It is the Word of God that records the crucial advice given to us by the Lord Jesus Christ Himself:

"Watch . . . and pray . . . that you may be accounted worthy to escape all these things" (Lk. 21:36).

"Occupy till I come" (Lk. 19:13).

"Even so, come, Lord Jesus" (Rev. 22:20).

Chapter 2

The Tribulation

CHAPTER TWO

THE TRIBULATION

A person who loses sight of Israel and her role in history, and the final consummation of all things has an erroneous view of history. A person cannot believe the Bible literally — especially Matthew, Chapter 24; Luke, Chapter 21; and Romans, Chapter 11 — and still hold to the liberal and humanistic view that man is slowly progressing through evolutionary stages until he finally ushers in a utopia, the Golden Age.

To the contrary, the Bible teaches that the world is rushing headlong toward a cataclysmic consummation of things as we know them. Prior to this event, the Church will be removed, Israel will be restored to the Land, Gentile dominion will be replaced, and the kingdoms of this world will become the kingdoms of our God.

It is with this in mind that the Christian sees the world. Every blade of grass, every grain of sand, every funeral, and every political and military move regarding Israel is seen in the light of the fall of man and God's restoration of all things. The Christian, therefore, is an optimist.

The world sees history as going nowhere; its existence is meaningless. Therefore, there is no Hope. This pessimism is reflected in our modern movies, rock music, and most modern art, which portrays a meaningless, purposeless Universe. This whole world view can be summed up by the lack of content in *"abstract painting,"* which is supposed to mirror the thinking of Twentieth Century man, that the world, the Universe, is nothing more than a product of chance. Is it any wonder the unregenerate person lives in hopelessness and fear?

GOD'S UNFOLDING PLAN

It has been said that the Old Testament is the New Testament concealed and the New Testament is the Old Testament revealed. Therefore, we must start with the Old Testament to understand the present world situation. Again, the future of the Church and the restoration of Israel as a Nation can be seen only in the light of the unfolding Revelation from Genesis through Malachi.

In the beginning God placed man in the Garden of Eden to restore and rule that which had been lost through Satan's rebellion. However, Adam, too, as a free moral agent, failed the test of obedience to God, which resulted in both a curse and a Blessing:

"And I will put enmity between you and the woman, and between your seed and her Seed; it (Christ) *shall bruise your head, and you shall bruise His Heel"* (Gen. 3:15).

This promise of a coming Redeemer was partially fulfilled at the coming of Christ and will be completed at the destruction of Satan at the end of the Millennium (Rom. 16:20; Heb. 2:14; Rev. 20:7-11). Ever since this Prophecy was pronounced, Satan has attempted to thwart God's Plan. He has murdered every suspected *"seed"* of woman (Gen. 4:8; Ex. 1:22; Mat. 2:16), has attempted to produce a mongrel race through intermarriage of fallen angels with the *"daughters of men"* (Gen. 6:4), and has tried to eliminate the people of God through genocide (Esther 3:13). His final act was to tempt Jesus to fall down and worship him (Lk. 4:1-13). Satan's battle against God's Anointed has raged continually through the centuries. It has been termed correctly the *"conflict of the ages."*

Later God predicted that the promised *"Seed"* would come through a particular branch of the race. Abraham of Ur of the Chaldees was chosen for this particular honour.

"Now the LORD had said unto Abram, Get thee out of your country, and from your kindred, and from your father's house, unto a land that I will show you:

"AND I WILL MAKE OF YOU A GREAT NATION, and I will bless you, and make your name great; and you shall be a blessing.

". . . AND IN YOU SHALL ALL FAMILIES OF THE EARTH BE BLESSED" (Gen. 12:1-3).

"And when Abram was ninety years old and nine, the LORD appeared to Abram, and said unto him, I am the Almighty God; walk before Me, and be thou perfect.

"And I will make My Covenant between Me and you, and will multiply you exceedingly.

". . . BEHOLD, MY COVENANT IS WITH YOU, AND YOU SHALL BE A FATHER OF MANY NATIONS.

"Neither shall your name any more be called Abram, but your name shall be Abraham; for a father of many nations have I made you.

"AND I WILL GIVE UNTO YOU, AND TO YOUR SEED AFTER YOU, THE LAND WHEREIN YOU ARE A STRANGER, ALL THE LAND OF CANAAN, FOR AN EVERLASTING POSSESSION; and I will be their God" (Gen. 17:1-2, 4-5, 8).

"All the nations of the Earth shall be blessed in him

[Abraham]" — (Gen. 18:18).

"YOUR SEED SHALL BE AS THE DUST OF THE EARTH, and you shall spread abroad to the west, and to the east, and to the north, and to the south: AND IN YOU AND IN YOUR SEED SHALL ALL THE FAMILIES OF THE EARTH BE BLESSED" (Gen. 28:14).

The New Testament reaffirms these promises (Gal. 3:8; Acts 3:25). Abraham's seed was to become a great Nation, it would produce the *"Seed"* of the woman, it would be a witness to the heathen nations of the True God Jehovah as opposed to their false gods, and would serve as an example of God's Blessing. Also included in the Abrahamic Covenant was a Promised Land that would stretch . . .

"from the river of Egypt [the Nile] *unto the great river, the river Euphrates"* (Gen. 15:18).

Israel has never yet occupied all this Land; however, God's Promise cannot fail. The time is coming when the whole Land promised to Abraham and his descendants will be occupied.

THE PLACE OF ISRAEL IN BIBLE PROPHECY

It was under Moses that the terms of the Covenant with Israel were set forth.

"And it shall come to pass, if you shall hearken diligently unto the Voice of the LORD your God, to observe and to do all His Commandments which I command you this day, that the LORD your God will set you on high above all nations of the Earth" (Deut. 28:1).

In the following Verses Moses, laid down the Blessings that would follow obedience. It is hard to understand why the Israelites, as well as people today, did not desire to walk in all God's Commandments and to enjoy the Blessings that would follow such obedience.

It took God only 14 verses to spell out the Blessings for obedience (Deut. 28:1-14) and 54 verses to spell out the curses for disobedience (Deut. 28:15-68).

God, Who knows the heart of man (Jn. 2:24-25), knew that the Israelites would not commit themselves to Him. But why give them warnings if He knew they would not keep them? For the same reason that He gives us warnings in the New Testament. The warnings were given that they would be without excuse and could never justify themselves by saying that they did not know (Rom. 1:18-32).

Like Lucifer and Adam, Israel failed to fulfill the conditions of the Covenant made with God (Deut., Chpts. 12 and 28), thus forfeiting the Divine Blessings.

After the death of King Solomon, the Nation began to fall; the kingdom was divided into North and South. In 721 B.C. the 10 Northern Tribes were destroyed, and the people scattered throughout the world. In 586 B.C., under King Nebuchadnezzar, the Southern Kingdom went into Babylonian Captivity and only a remnant returned to the Land. From this time on, Israel as a sovereign Nation ceased to exist. This was a partial fulfillment of the Prophecy:

> *"And it shall come to pass, that as the LORD rejoiced over you to do you good, and to multiply you; so the LORD will rejoice over you to destroy you, and to bring you to nought; and you shall be plucked from off the land where you go to possess it.*
>
> *"And the LORD shall scatter you among all people, from the one end of the Earth even unto the other. . . .*
>
> *"And among these nations shall you find no ease, neither shall the sole of your foot have rest: but the LORD shall give you there a trembling heart, and failing of eyes, and sorrow of mind:*
>
> *"And your life shall hang in doubt before you; and you shall fear day and night, and shall have none assurance of your life"* (Deut. 28:63-66).

The final dispersion and fulfillment of this Prophecy came when the Jews rejected the Lord Jesus Christ as their Messiah and Jerusalem was conquered by Gentiles. Jesus foretold:

> *"And Jerusalem shall be trodden down of the Gentiles, until the times of the Gentiles be fulfilled"* (Lk. 21:24).

"Until the times of the Gentiles be fulfilled," meant that Israel would be oppressed under Gentile dominion, and Jerusalem would be controlled by Gentile nations.

This Prophecy of the final dispersion of the Jews, correlating with Deuteronomy, Chapter 28, was literally fulfilled when Jerusalem was surrounded by the Roman armies under General Titus in A.D. 70. The city was completely sacked, and not one stone of Herod's Temple was left standing, just as Jesus had prophesied (Lk. 21:6, 20, 24). The Gentiles took over the Land and controlled it for 1,900 years.

THE WRATH OF GOD

Just as Deuteronomy, Chapter 28 prophesied, the history of the Jews has been a history of wandering, persecution, murder, and hatred. The Jews have been hated by the Church and the world as being the murderers of Jesus (Acts 2:23). Yet they were not alone in their guilt. We too were and are just as guilty. Millions of people still cry:

"Crucify Him, crucify Him" (Lk. 23:21)

. . . rather than have Him to rule over them (cf. I Sam. 8:4-9).

Let us not be too harsh on Israel, however, because the Wrath of God from the beginning applied to all nations that failed God.

Listen to the Apostle Paul:

"For the Wrath of God is revealed from Heaven against all ungodliness and unrighteousness of men, who hold the truth in unrighteousness" (Rom. 1:18).

But a person may say, *"I thought God was a God of Mercy."*

He is a Merciful God, but He is also a Just God. He cannot go back on His Word.

"God . . . cannot lie" (Titus 1:2).

If God gives a Promise or a Prophecy, He must keep that word, else He would not be God and we could not trust Him (Num. 23:19; I Sam. 15:29). God gave the Israelites a conditional Covenant, and they broke that Covenant. God has never broken, and never will break, His part of any Covenant:

"There has not failed one word of all His good Promise" (I Ki. 8:56).

Just as Israel's failure resulted in a forfeiture of God's Blessings and the punishment prophesied in Deuteronomy, Chapter 28, so, likewise, the Gentile world has failed to worship God:

"When they knew God, they glorified Him not as God,

neither were thankful; but became vain in their imaginations, and their foolish heart was darkened" (Rom. 1:21).

That is, their reasoning became vain. Consequently, the Gentiles also abide under the Wrath of God.

"God is angry with the wicked every day" (Ps. 7:11).

This subject of the Wrath of God is sorely missing from our pulpits today. Today's emphasis is the positive Blessings of God; however, only when this is balanced with the Warnings of God will our life conform to that *"Blessed Hope."*

For example, John 3:36 is often quoted for assurance of Salvation, especially the first half of the Verse:

"He who believes on the Son has Everlasting Life."

True, yet seldom is the latter half ever quoted, and if it is, it is usually de-emphasized. Listen to its warning:

"And he who believes [obey] *not the Son shall not see life; but the WRATH OF GOD ABIDES ON HIM."*

When a person is not Born-Again and does not walk obediently in the Light of God's Word, he is living in a state of disobedience and the Wrath of God abides continually upon him.

This wrath, however, is not to be confused with the . . .

"WRATH to come" (Lk. 3:7).

The *"wrath to come"* will not be poured out on the Church, for by the Blood of Jesus . . .

"we shall be Saved from WRATH through him" (Rom. 5:9).

"God has not appointed us to WRATH, but to obtain Salvation by our Lord Jesus Christ" (I Thess. 5:9).

It is the lot of the Church . . .

"to wait for His Son from Heaven, Whom He raised from the dead, even Jesus, which delivered us from the WRATH to come" (I Thess. 1:10; Mat. 3:7).

The Day of the Lord will be a horrifying, terrifying day for the world (Isa. 13:9-11; Joel 3:9-17), but a glorious day for the Blood-washed, Blood-bought Saints of God.

KING NEBUCHADNEZZAR'S IMAGE

Just as we must understand the place of Israel in Prophecy and the Wrath of God, so also, to study the Great Tribulation, we must understand the Prophecies of Daniel and Revelation.

King Nebuchadnezzar was given a dream so that he might know the things that would befall his kingdom after his death. The dream also was a revelation of world empires that would come after him.

King Nebuchadnezzar saw . . .

> "a great image, whose brightness was excellent . . . and the form thereof was terrible.
> "THIS IMAGE'S HEAD WAS OF FINE GOLD, HIS BREAST AND HIS ARMS OF SILVER, HIS BELLY AND HIS THIGHS OF BRASS.
> "HIS LEGS OF IRON, HIS FEET PART OF IRON AND PART OF CLAY.
> "a Stone was cut out without hands, which smote the image upon his feet that were of iron and clay, and broke them to pieces.
> "Then was the iron, the clay, the brass, the silver, and the gold, broken to pieces together, and became like the chaff of the summer threshingfloors; and the wind carried them away, that no place was found for them: and the Stone . . . became a great mountain, and filled the whole Earth" (Dan. 2:31-35).

The great image that Nebuchadnezzar saw had five parts, each containing a specific metal: gold, silver, brass, iron, and clay. A Stone not made with hands appeared and smote the image on the feet, breaking them into pieces. The broken pieces became like chaff, carried away with the wind.

Jesus Christ is that Stone made without hands (Isa. 8:14; Ps. 118:22; Acts 4:11). Notice that the Stone did not strike the head, which represented King Nebuchadnezzar and the Babylonian Empire. Nor did it strike the body of silver. Rather it struck the feet of iron and clay.

The Prophet Daniel revealed to King Nebuchadnezzar the meaning of the dream. He told him:

> "You, O king . . . are this HEAD OF GOLD.
> "And after you shall rise ANOTHER KINGDOM INFERIOR

*to you, and ANOTHER THIRD KINGDOM OF BRASS, which
shall bear rule over all the Earth.*

*"And the FOURTH KINGDOM SHALL BE STRONG AS
IRON: forasmuch as iron breaks in pieces and subdues all
things: and as iron that breaks all these, shall it break in pieces
and bruise.*

*"And whereas you saw the feet and toes, PART OF THE
POTTERS' CLAY, AND PART OF IRON, the kingdom shall be
divided; but there shall be in it of the strength of the iron, forasmuch as you saw the iron mixed with miry clay.*

*"And as the toes of the feet were part of iron, and part of
clay, so the kingdom shall be partly strong, and partly broken.*

*"And whereas you saw iron mixed with miry clay, they shall
mingle themselves with the seed of men: but they shall not
cleave one to another, even as iron is not mixed with clay.*

*"And IN THE DAYS OF THESE KINGS SHALL THE GOD
OF HEAVEN SET UP A KINGDOM, WHICH SHALL NEVER
BE DESTROYED: and the kingdom shall not be left to other
people, but it shall break in pieces and consume all these kingdoms, and it shall stand forever.*

*"Forasmuch as you saw that THE STONE WAS CUT OUT
OF THE MOUNTAIN WITHOUT HANDS, AND THAT IT
BROKE IN PIECES THE IRON, THE BRASS, THE CLAY, THE
SILVER, AND THE GOLD, the great God has made known to
the king what shall come to pass hereafter: and the dream is
certain, and the interpretation thereof sure"* (Dan. 2:37-45).

The great image of King Nebuchadnezzar consisted of five different
substances, representing five different world empires: gold (Babylonian
Empire), silver (Medo-Persian Empire), brass (Greek Empire), iron
(Roman Empire), iron and clay (Revised Roman Empire). This last, the
Revised Roman Empire, corresponding to the 10 toes of King
Nebuchadnezzar's image will be composed of 10 kingdoms.

1. GOLD (Dan. 2:32, 35, 38) — Babylon. During his extended reign,
   King Nebuchadnezzar besieged Jerusalem, the Holy City, three
   times. He destroyed her walls, burned her great Temple, carted
   away her great treasures, and carried away her people. He
   also defeated the Moabites, the Philistines, the Amorites, the
   Assyrians; besieged Tyre; and invaded Egypt. He made Babylon
   one of the wonders of the ancient world. His great military genius
   and the great wealth he extracted from conquered land brought

him to the zenith of a world empire. Israel was oppressed by Babylon for 70 years.

2. SILVER (Dan. 2:32, 35, 39) — Medo-Persia. The Medes and Persians succeeded Babylon as a world empire at the end of the seventy-year captivity for the Jews. The two nations making up the dual kingdom are symbolized in Nebuchadnezzar's image by the two arms. This kingdom was inferior to Babylon, just as silver is inferior to gold.

3. BRASS (Dan. 2:32, 35, 39) — Greece. The Greek Empire came to be a world empire *c.* 331 B.C. with Alexander the Great as its head. Alexander conquered all the territory that had belonged to both Babylon and Medo-Persia, along with India. When Alexander died at the mere age of 32, his empire was divided into four parts, each of his four generals taking a share: Ptolemy (Egypt), Seleucus I (Syria and Persia), Lysimachus (Asia Minor), and Cassander (Macedonia). (This was foretold in Dan. 7:6; 8:8; 22.)

4. IRON (Dan. 2:33-35, 40) — Rome. The Old Roman Empire is depicted in King Nebuchadnezzar's image by the legs of iron. The two legs represent East and West. As a World empire, this kingdom continued until *c.* A.D. 476.

5. IRON AND CLAY (Dan. 2:33-35, 41) — Revised Rome. This is man's last world empire, made up of 10 kingdoms, symbolized by 10 toes in King Nebuchadnezzar's image. It will arise out of the Old Roman Empire territory, which includes the modern day countries of England, France, Belgium, Switzerland, Holland, Spain, Portugal, Italy, Austria, Hungary, Romania, Yugoslavia, Bulgaria, Albania, Greece, Turkey, Syria, Lebanon, Egypt, Iraq, Iran, Libya, Algeria, Tunisia, and Morocco. These many countries will be reduced to a 10-kingdom confederacy before the Antichrist is revealed (Dan. 7:7-8, 23-24; Rev. 17:10-13).

SEVENTY WEEKS OF YEARS

We recognize that there are many diverse thoughts in regard to the interpretation of Daniel's 70 weeks of years. Yet we honestly believe that we must, after much prayer and study, come to a place where we can stand confidently in our Prophetic posture.

Archimedes, the inventor of the pulley and lever, once said: *"Give me a place to stand and I will move the world."* (The fulcrum and lever was an ancient engineering method of distributing weight in order to lift extremely heavy objects.)

The Christian who fails to find a place to stand in his Doctrine will never move anyone for Christ.

Jesus' commendation of John the Baptist illustrates this point:

> *"What went you out . . . to see? A reed shaken with the wind?"* (Lk. 7:24).

No! John the Baptist was not shaken by every wind and doctrine. He knew where he stood and was willing to stake his life on the genuineness of his belief. Because of his unwavering and uncompromising stand, he struck fear in King Herod and the religious hypocrites of his day, and gained a hearing from the disenchanted and disillusioned.

It is the same today. People are tired of vacillating, compromising religious and political leaders who no longer stand for anything, but fall for everything. People are looking for something absolute, something concrete on which to build their life. They are tired of clarifying their values, and desire to return to the old paths of absolutes. It is the religious and political leaders that are taking a moral stand who are gaining an audience.

The Prophecy of the 70 weeks of years was given under unusual circumstances. The Prophet Daniel and his people had been taken into Babylonian Captivity and the Holy City, Jerusalem, had been desecrated and sacked (II Chron. 36:17-21). The Prophet Daniel had learned from studying the parchments that the Prophet Jeremiah, years ago, had written twice in his Prophecy that Israel would be in captivity for 70 years (Jer. 25:11-12; 29:10). Calculating from the fall of Jerusalem and the carrying away of the captives to his present day, Daniel discovered that the 70 years were almost ended and it was time for his people to be returned to their Homeland.

Immediately upon realizing the significance of this Revelation for his people and for the Holy City, Daniel set himself to prayer and supplication before God, confessing his sins and the sins of his people, which had resulted in this great calamity.

While Daniel was seeking the face of God, through prayer and supplication, the Angel Gabriel appeared to him and began to reveal God's Plan for the future. Gabriel told Daniel to . . .

> *"understand the matter, and consider the Vision"* (Dan. 9:23).

He went on to tell him:

> *"SEVENTY WEEKS ARE DETERMINED UPON YOUR PEOPLE AND UPON YOUR HOLY CITY, to finish the*

transgression, and to make an end of sins, and to make reconciliation for iniquity, and to bring in everlasting Righteousness, and to seal up the Vision and Prophecy, and to anoint the Most Holy.

"Know therefore and understand, that FROM THE GOING FORTH OF THE COMMANDMENT TO RESTORE AND TO BUILD JERUSALEM UNTO THE MESSIAH THE PRINCE SHALL BE SEVEN WEEKS, AND THREESCORE AND TWO WEEKS. . . .

"And after threescore and two weeks shall Messiah be cut off, but not for Himself: and the people of the prince who shall come shall destroy the city and the sanctuary. . . .

"AND HE SHALL CONFIRM THE COVENANT WITH MANY FOR ONE WEEK: and in the midst of the week he shall cause the sacrifice and the oblation to cease, and for the overspreading of abominations he shall make it desolate" (Dan. 9:24-27).

The *first* thing we notice is that . . .

"seventy weeks are determined."

In other words, they have been fixed and planned by God, and therefore cannot be changed.

The *second* thing we notice is that the weeks concern . . .

"your people and . . . your holy city."

No Gentiles are mentioned here. In other words, this does not in any way concern the Church, but it relates specifically to the restoration of Israel to the Promised Land.

The *third* thing we notice is that the weeks are divided into a trilogy of events: (1) seven weeks of years (49 years), (2) 62 weeks of years (434 years), and (3) one week of years (seven years) — a total of 70 weeks of years (490 years).

The *fourth* thing we notice is that the weeks begin with . . .

"the commandment to restore and to build Jerusalem."

Three decrees for the restoration of Jerusalem actually were given.

1. The first decree was given in the first year of King Cyrus of Persia (Ezra 1:1-4; Chpt. 3; Chpt. 8; Isa. 45:1-4; 46:11). Cyrus reigned

for nine years and then was succeeded by his son, Cambyses, who reigned for seven years. During Cambyses' reign, work on the Temple ceased (Ezra 4:1-24).

2. The second decree was given by Darius the Mede, who reigned 35 years. In the second year of his reign he reactivated Cyrus' decree. Consequently, the Temple was completed in the sixth year of Darius, but the city was not restored.

3. The third decree was given by Artaxerxes about 20 years into his reign (c. 445 B.C.). It was at this time that Nehemiah rebuilt the walls of Jerusalem which had fallen down.

And so, we begin the calculation of the 490 years from the time the decree to rebuild Jerusalem was issued to Nehemiah in 445 B.C. (Neh. 2:1-9). It was hearing of the broken down walls and burned gates of Jerusalem that stirred Nehemiah to a state of prayer and fasting for Jerusalem and the nation. As the Jewish cupbearer for Artaxerxes, the king, Nehemiah petitioned the king:

> *"If it please the king, and if your servant have found favour in your sight, that you would send me unto Judah, unto the city of my fathers' sepulchres, that I may build it"* (Neh. 2:5).

The king's response was . . .

> *"For how long shall your journey be? and when will you return? So it pleased the king to send me; and I set him a time . . . And the king granted me, according to the good hand of my God upon me"* (Neh. 2:6-8).

At his request the king gave Nehemiah an official letter to give to the provisional governor of Jerusalem allowing him safe passage and another letter permitting him timber to rebuild the walls.

The most significant part here, besides the command to build the city, is that it took place in the twentieth year of Artaxerxes. History tells us that the date of Artaxerxes' ascension to the throne of Persia was 465 B.C. The twentieth year of his reign would place the date of this decree at 445 B.C. Here we have the beginning of the 70 weeks.

The Angel told Daniel:

> *"Know therefore and understand, that from the going forth of the Commandment to restore and to build Jerusalem unto*

*the Messiah the Prince shall be SEVEN WEEKS, and THREE-
SCORE AND TWO WEEKS: the street shall be built again,
and the wall, even in troublous times"* (Dan. 9:25).

Again the Angel exhorted Daniel to *"know and understand"* the events
that were about to transpire. Through the help of the Holy Spirit (cf. 1
Cor. 2:9-14) Daniel had already understood Jeremiah's Prophecy of 70
years to be that of Israel's captivity in Babylon. This was indicated by his
going to prayer and fasting after reading Jeremiah's Prophecy.

We too would have a clearer Revelation of God's Word if we spent
more time in prayer and fasting and seeking God's Revelation of Scripture rather than spending so much time in reading commentaries and other
related extra-Biblical sources. Many of these were written by uninspired
and unanointed men. They may be scholarly, but many of these commen-
tators do not believe in predictive Prophecy, nor have they ever experienced the Baptism in the Holy Spirit.

While Daniel was instant in prayer, the Angel interrupted him to inform
him that he was to understand that Israel's restoration would not be complete until another 70 weeks of years had passed.

The word *"weeks"* comes from a Hebrew word meaning *"years."*
The Jews were very familiar with the term *"seven years"* as it was an
integral part of their history and life-style. They were to till their fields for
six years and allow it to lie fallow on the seventh year (Lev. 25:3-4). Also,
they were to observe the Year of Jubilee (Lev. 25:8-13). This was to be a
year of rest for the soil and was to take place at the end of seven sabbaths
of years, or 49 years. During the fiftieth year not only was the land to lie
fallow, but slaves were to be set free, debts canceled, and possessions
returned. This Year of Jubilee was ushered in with trumpet blasts and a
proclamation of liberty throughout the Land.

There is no Scriptural evidence that Israel ever observed the Year of
Jubilee. There is at least one Scripture, though, that indicates one reason
for Israel's 70 years of captivity was her violations of the Sabbath year.
According to II Chronicles 36:21 Israel was removed from the Land that it
might rest for 70 years. The writer said that Israel was carried off into the
Babylonian Captivity . . .

*"To fulfill the Word of the LORD by the mouth of Jeremiah,
UNTIL THE LAND HAD ENJOYED HER SABBATHS: for as
long as she lay desolate she kept Sabbath, to fulfill threescore
and ten years"* (II Chron. 36:21).

Someone has observed that if a person does not pay his tithe, God will have it in other ways. *God will have His Tithe.* Similarly, God meant for the Land to rest even if He had to remove the stubborn people off into captivity for 70 years!

Now that we understand something of the concept of a Sabbath of years, or a sabbatical, we might well ask ourselves, *"How long is a year?"* The best reference for determining the number of days in a Biblical year is the Scriptures themselves. Our first clue is Genesis 7:11 —

> *"In the six hundredth year of Noah's life, in the SECOND MONTH, the seventeenth day of the month, the same day were all the fountains of the great deep broken up"* (Gen. 7:11).

Now let us notice Genesis 8:4 —

> *"And the ark rested in the SEVENTH MONTH, on the seventeenth day of the month . . ."* (Gen. 8:4).

Simple subtraction tells us that the Flood lasted an even five months, or 150 days (Gen. 7:24; 8:13), meaning 30 days to a month, 360 days to a year. So the Biblical definition of a year is 12 lunar months or 360 days.

Our second clue is found in Daniel's Prophecy. The Angel mentioned a covenant of one week (Dan. 9:27). One week is a week of years, or seven years. In the middle of this week, or three and one half years, the sacrifices will cease and the abomination of desolation will be set up. John the Revelator, speaking of this event in Revelation 12:6, mentioned the time as . . .

> *"a thousand two hundred and threescore days"*

. . . that is, 1,260 days, which is three and one half years. John, in Revelation 13:5, called it . . .

> *"forty and two months"*

. . . which is, again, 1,260 days or three and one half years.

These comparative Passages indicate conclusively that the Scriptures regard a year as 360 days.

Again, Daniel's 70 weeks of years are divided into three divisions: seven, 62, and one week.

Dating from Nisan 1, 445 B.C., the date the decree to build Jerusalem was issued to Nehemiah, to the Triumphal Entry of Christ into Jerusalem on

Palm Sunday, five days before His Crucifixion in A.D. 33, would be 483 years, or 69 weeks of years. This would mark the date of the Messiah's manifestation as the *"Prince"* of Daniel 9:25. This was the day that Jesus rode into Jerusalem on the *"foal of an ass"* (Zech.9:9) and offered Himself as the *"Prince"* or *"King"* of Israel (Lk. 19:28-44).

Upon entering Jerusalem, Jesus rebuked the Pharisees for protesting the loud cries of . . .

> *"Blessed be the King Who comes in the Name of the Lord: peace in Heaven, and glory in the highest"* (Lk. 19:38).

Jesus confirmed the cries of the multitude and rebuked the Pharisees by stating that if the people did not hail Him as King . . .

> *"the stones would immediately cry out"* (Lk. 19:40)!

Knowing the Jews' coming rejection of Him as King and the resultant coming destruction of the Holy City and the Holy People, Jesus began to lament:

> *"If you had known, even you, at least in this your day, the things which belong unto your peace! but now they are hid from your eyes.*
> *"For the days shall come upon you, that your enemies shall cast a trench about you, and compass you round, and keep you in on every side,*
> *"And shall lay you even with the ground, and your children within you; and they shall not leave in you one stone upon another; BECAUSE YOU KNEW NOT THE TIME OF YOUR VISITATION"* (Lk. 19:42-44).

What time was it? The literal fulfillment of the Prophecy of their long-awaited Messiah, the climax of the 69 weeks of years. However, due to the rejection of their *"Messiah the Prince,"* the *"things which belong unto your peace"* were now *"hid from your eyes"* (cf. Dan. 9:24; Lk. 19:42-44). Their rejection was due to their not knowing the *"time of your visitation."* If they had studied Daniel 9:24-27 carefully and prayerfully, as we are doing, much confusion, destruction, and sorrow could have been avoided.

Such tragedy, such confusion, such sorrow still continues. He still comes to millions whose lives, families, and nations are being destroyed because of a lack of knowledge (Hos. 4:6). The signs of His Coming are all around us, still millions of persons are blinded by self-will and refuse to discern the *"time of your visitation"*!

Our problem is the same as theirs — a heart problem. Too many persons come to Jesus for what they can get out of Him: forgiveness without Repentance, Cadillacs without commitment, healing without pain, Salvation without sacrifice, and Hope without Him.

Jesus analyzed the heart of the multitude and concluded that He would not commit Himself unto them:

> *"Now when He was in Jerusalem at the Passover, on the Feast Day, many believed in His Name, when they saw the Miracles which He did.*
> *"BUT JESUS DID NOT COMMIT HIMSELF UNTO THEM, BECAUSE HE KNEW ALL MEN,*
> *"And needed not that any should testify of man: for He knew what was in man"* (Jn. 2:23-25).

We cannot hide our real motive from God, for He . . .

> *"is a discerner of the thoughts and intents of the heart"* (Heb. 4:12).

The Jews were looking for a King that would overthrow their Roman oppressors and once again restore greatness to Israel as in former times. However, when they discovered that His Way to greatness and, consequently, the Kingdom was through suffering and death, their real motives were manifested:

> *"From that time many of His Disciples went back, and walked no more with Him"* (Jn. 6:66).

And so, the first seven weeks, or 49 years, take us to the time when the city and the wall were rebuilt under Nehemiah. Then, after 62 weeks, or 434 years, the Messiah, Jesus Christ, was cut off at Calvary.

At this point in time, between the 69th and 70th week, the prophetic time clock was suspended. The intervening period, between the Crucifixion and the Tribulation, sometimes called the *"Great Parenthesis,"* has been the Church Age, or a period when God no longer has dealt with Israel as a Nation.

Jerusalem was destroyed in A.D. 70 by the Roman army. Since that time, Israel has been dispersed among the nations of the world, and God has been calling out a Church, the Body of Christ, to fulfill His Divine

Plan. When the Church is raptured, God once again will deal with National Israel in the last unfulfilled week of Daniel's Prophecy, commonly called the Tribulation:

> *"Alas! For that day is great, so that none is like it: it is even the TIME OF JACOB'S TROUBLE; but he shall be Saved out of it"* (Jer. 30:7).

Naturally the question arises: On what basis do we fix a gap between the 69th and 70th weeks that has continued for 1,900 years?

H. A. Ironside points out that there are many illustrations of gaps found in Scripture; therefore, a gap here is not unusual.

To illustrate: Isaiah 61:1-2 pictures one of the most obvious gaps in Scripture. Isaiah 61:2 says:

> *"To proclaim the acceptable Year of the LORD, and the day of vengeance of our God."*

Over 700 years later, Jesus of Nazareth was given this portion of Scripture to read in a Synagogue in Nazareth. Jesus read Isaiah 61:1, but only *half* of Isaiah 61:2. He said:

> *"The Spirit of the Lord is upon Me, because He has anointed Me to preach the Gospel to the poor; He has sent Me to heal the brokenhearted, to preach deliverance to the captives, and recovering of sight to the blind, to set at liberty them who are bruised,*
> *"To preach the acceptable Year of the Lord.*
> *"AND HE CLOSED THE BOOK, AND HE GAVE IT AGAIN TO THE MINISTER, AND SAT DOWN . . .*
> *"And He began to say unto them, THIS DAY IS THIS SCRIPTURE FULFILLED IN YOUR EARS"* (Lk. 4:18-21).

Why did He read only part of Isaiah 61:2? Because the rest of the Verse . . .

> *"and the day of vengeance of our God"*

. . . referred not to His First Advent, but to His Second Advent. It would not be fulfilled for another 1,900 years!

To illustrate again: Daniel prophesied that the *"prince"* who would come, meaning the Antichrist, would . . .

"confirm the covenant with many for one week: and in the midst of the week he shall cause the sacrifice and the oblation to cease, and for the overspreading of abominations he shall make it desolate" (Dan. 9:27).

Actually the Book of Daniel has four Passages that use this term — Daniel 8:13; 9:27; 11:31; and, 12:11. In the first two instances, Antiochus Epiphanes (reigned *c.* 175-164 B.C.) is depicted. This Syrian king did away with proper sacrifices and offered swine on the altar in Zerubbabel's Temple. (Of course, to the Jews swine were unclean and, therefore, an abomination. See Lev. 11:7-8; Deut. 14:8.) The presence of this abomination in the Sanctuary made it unfit for worship. Moreover, it was abhorrent and detestable in God's sight. Those that worshiped at such altars . . .

"became as detestable" (Hos. 9:10, NASB).

Jesus quoted from Daniel in reply to the Disciples' inquiry as to a sign announcing His Coming (Mat. 24:3). In referring to the . . .

"abomination of desolation, spoken of by Daniel the Prophet . . . in the Holy Place" (Mat.24:15)

. . . Jesus was saying to the Disciples and to Israel that when they saw this take place in the future, it would invoke on God's part the greatest time of tribulation that the world has ever seen or ever will see (Mat. 24:21).

This is evidence enough that a gap exists between Daniel's 69th week when the Messiah is *"cut off"* (Dan. 9:26) and that 70th week when the Antichrist . . .

"shall confirm the covenant with many for one week: and in the midst of the week he shall cause the sacrifice and the oblation to cease, and for the overspreading of abominations he shall make it desolate" (Dan. 9:27).

Other gaps in Scripture that may be mentioned for study are Isaiah 9:6-7; Zechariah 9:9-10; and, Acts 2:16-21.

GOD'S PURPOSE IN THE SEVENTY WEEKS OF YEARS

Keeping in mind that God is dealing with the Nation of Israel and the Holy City, let us examine the Purpose of God to be fulfilled in the 70 weeks of years.

"Seventy weeks are determined upon your people and upon your holy city, TO FINISH THE TRANSGRESSION, and TO MAKE AN END OF SINS, AND TO MAKE RECONCILIATION FOR INIQUITY, and TO BRING IN EVERLASTING RIGHTEOUSNESS, and TO SEAL UP THE VISION AND PROPHECY, and TO ANOINT THE MOST HOLY" (Dan. 9:24).

1. TO FINISH THE TRANSGRESSION. The word *"transgression"* means *"to revolt, to rebel,"* and refers to those who reject God's Authority. The obvious meaning is that Israel's sin of rebellion and apostasy will be brought to an end within the 70 weeks.

2. TO MAKE AN END OF SINS. Keil states that the word *"make"* *"does not denote the finishing or ending of sins,"* rather *"they are altogether removed out of the sight of God, altogether set aside."* Young states that *"make"* means the sins are reserved for punishment (Job 14:17; cf. Deut. 32:34). To be sure, their sins will be brought to an end in Judgment.

3. TO MAKE RECONCILIATION FOR INIQUITY. *"Reconciliation"* here means *"to pardon, to blot out by means of a sin offering, to forgive."* Obviously, this is a reference to the Cross of Christ (II Cor. 5:19). As a Nation, Israel has not yet experienced this reconciliation to God, but they will at the Second Coming of Christ.

4. TO BRING IN EVERLASTING RIGHTEOUSNESS. While Christ's First Coming provided a Righteous ground for God's Justification of sinners, the many Messianic Passages indicate a Righteousness applied to the Earth at the Second Coming.

   "Nevertheless we, according to His Promise, look for New Heavens and a New Earth, wherein dwells Righteousness" (II Pet. 3:13; cf. Jer. 9:6-7; 11:2-5).

5. TO SEAL UP THE VISION AND PROPHECY. The word *"seal"* means to set aside, that no more is to be added, that what has been written will be confirmed at the appointed time. This does not mean, as some people suppose, that all Prophecy has ended or that the sins and iniquities of Israel have ceased. It means, rather, that the Prophecy is complete within itself.

6. TO ANOINT THE MOST HOLY. The Prophecy carries us up to the First and Second Advents of Christ.

(For further study, we recommend the Jimmy Swaggart Bible Commentary on *The Book of Daniel,* available through Jimmy Swaggart Ministries.)

THE COMING ANTICHRIST

There is a natural break between Daniel 9:26 and Daniel 9:27. The first half of Verse 26 mentions that *after* 62 weeks (in addition to the initial seven weeks, or *after* 69 weeks) the Messiah is cut off. We realize that this is history, as the Lord Jesus Christ was *"cut off"* at Calvary.

But when we look at the second half of Verse 26 and Verse 27, we see immediately that it is talking about events of the 70th week. Actually we are given a panoramic view of the entire 70th week.

"And the people of the prince who shall come shall destroy the city and the sanctuary; and the end thereof shall be with a flood, and unto the end of the war desolations are determined.
"AND HE SHALL CONFIRM THE COVENANT WITH MANY FOR ONE WEEK: AND IN THE MIDST OF THE WEEK HE SHALL CAUSE THE SACRIFICE AND THE OBLATION TO CEASE, AND FOR THE OVERSPREADING OF ABOMINATIONS HE SHALL MAKE IT DESOLATE" (Dan. 9:26-27).

Who is the *"he"* of Daniel 9:27?

It cannot be Jesus the Christ, because He did not confirm a covenant with anyone according to the Bible or secular history. Some persons suppose that Jesus confirmed a covenant with the Jews at His Baptism and was *"cut off"* three years later at His Crucifixion. Yet there is no record of any covenant made with the Jews, and even if there was, what happened to the second half of the *"week"* of this alleged covenant? History records that it was somewhere around 38 years before the Holy City and the Temple were destroyed, and the sacrifice and oblation ceased, and not at the time of the Crucifixion. Besides, Jesus' Blood is called . . .

"the Blood of the EVERLASTING COVENANT" (Heb. 13:20).

It cannot be General Titus or Emperor Nero. Titus did not confirm a covenant with the Jews and then break it in the middle of the *"week."* Again, these events happened between the 69th and 70th *"week"* of Daniel's Prophecy. Furthermore, the Jews were scattered throughout the world after the Roman destruction of the Holy City. So, the *"prince"* could not confirm a covenant with the Jews until they are brought back into their

Land. Jerusalem and the Temple must be restored before the seven-year covenant can be made. According to Daniel 9:27 the Temple will again be desolate in the middle of the *"week."* Since A.D. 70 the Temple has never been restored. So the fulfillment of Daniel 9:27 must still be future.

The Jews too must be restored to the Land. Jesus said:

> *"O Jerusalem, Jerusalem, you who kill the Prophets, and stone them which are sent unto you, how often would I have gathered your children together, even as a hen gathers her chickens under her wings, and you would not!*
> *"Behold, your house is left unto you desolate.*
> *"For I say unto you, you shall not see Me henceforth, till you shall say, Blessed is He Who comes in the Name of the Lord"* (Mat. 23:37-39).

It is obvious, then, that the 70th week remains to be fulfilled when God again deals with Israel as a Nation (Ezek., Chpt. 37). Then, in order for the events of Daniel 9:27 to transpire, it would be necessary for the Jews to be established in their Land and for the Temple to be in operation.

We conclude, then, that the *"he"* of Daniel 9:27 is the *"prince that shall come"* of Verse 26, the coming deceiver of Israel, the Antichrist. He will not appear before the world until the 10 kingdoms (Dan. 7:23-24) are formed within the Old Roman Empire and until after the Rapture of the Church (II Thess. 2:6-8). His *"week"* will be the last of Daniel's 70 weeks of Years — the 70th week. This *"week"* will comprise the time between the Rapture and the Second Coming of Christ, that time known as the Tribulation.

The terms of the covenant, or agreement, between the Antichrist and Israel are not clear. However, it will be a political alliance that will enable the Antichrist to gain power over the 10 kingdoms. Involved in the agreement will be the protection of Israel in her Homeland, the restoring of temporary peace and the promise of continued peace. The covenant, or agreement, will be set for seven years; that is, a *"week"* in Daniel's 70 weeks of years.

In the middle of this *"week,"* or after three and one half years, the Antichrist will break his covenant with Israel. He will invade Jerusalem, defile the Temple, and set himself up to be worshipped (Dan. 11:36-37; II Thess. 2:4). Jesus referred to this as the *"abomination of desolation"* (Mat. 24:15). While the Antichrist will use Babylon as his capital for the first three and one half years, he will rule from the Temple at Jerusalem for the last three and one half (Isa. 14:4-11; II Thess. 2:3-4).

The Apostle John used the term *"antichrist"* five times (I Jn. 2:18, 22;

4:3, II Jn., Vs. 7). Of the five references only one refers to a future Anti-christ (I Jn. 2:18). This future Antichrist will oppose Christ and all He stands for. The basic meaning of *"anti"* is to *"stand against or instead of."* The Antichrist, then, will be a person who will stand both in the place of Christ and in opposition to Him.

Although this singular person is referred to by many names in Scripture, he is generally known by four titles: the King of the North (Dan. 11:40), the Little Horn (Dan. 8:9), the Man of Sin (II Thess. 2:3), and the Beast (Rev. 13:1). In all three instances he is identified with the *"he"* of Daniel 9:27.

THE KING OF THE NORTH. In the Vision of Daniel, as recorded in Daniel, Chapter 8, we see a symbolic ram and he-goat, the ram being Medo-Persia and the he-goat being the Grecian Empire. The he-goat had his horn broken off, and in its place grew four horns. This relates to the death of Alexander the Great (*c*. 323 B.C.), founder of the Old Grecian Empire. After his death the kingdom was divided among his four generals: (1) Ptolemy took the area of Egypt, Arabia, and Palestine; (2) Cassander took Macedonia and Greece; (3) Lysimachus took the area of Thrace and Bithynia; (4) Seleucus I took Assyria. Today their territory would cover, generally, the areas of Egypt, Greece, Turkey, and Syria, respectively. These four kings began to war among themselves. These wars covered approximately 150 years and ended with the reign of Antiochus Epiphanes (reigned *c*. 175-164 B.C.). Now, it is a historical fact that Antiochus Epiphanes came out of Syria, one of the four kingdoms. In the height of his power he went into Jerusalem and desecrated the Temple, abused and killed the Priest of God, went to the Altar, upon which only Holy things and clean animals were sacrificed, and as an insult to Israel's God and the Holy worship, he slaughtered a swine upon the Altar. This was an abomination. But it was *not* the fulfillment of Daniel's Prophecy (Dan. 9:27; Mat. 24:15).

Antiochus Epiphanes was *a* King of the North, from Syria, and therefore was a *type* of Antichrist, but he was not that *"prince"* to come of which Daniel wrote (Dan. 9:27; 11:45).

In the Vision (Dan., Chpt. 11), the man of Syria is called the King of the North, and the man of Egypt is called the King of the South. Daniel 11:36-45 identifies the Antichrist as this King of the North, from Syria.

Several things are revealed about this King of the North (Dan. 11:36-39). He will do as he pleases. He will exalt and magnify himself above every god. He will speak great swelling words against the God of gods. He will prosper, as God allows, until *"the indignation be accomplished"* or the Tribulation ends. The Hebrew word for *"indignation"* is *zaam*, meaning *"fury."* This King of the North, from Syria, will be the last king before

God puts down sin on the Earth (Rev. 21:3-7). This man, the King of the North, will not regard the God of his Fathers, nor will he have any interest or regard for *"the desire of women."* He will be perverted, self-centered, and reprobate.

THE LITTLE HORN. When the one great horn of the he-goat was broken and four horns took its place, Daniel said:

"Out of one of them came forth A LITTLE HORN" (Dan. 8:9).

This little horn grew exceedingly great and expanded toward the south and the east and the Pleasant Land, meaning Israel (Ps. 106:24; Jer. 3:19; Ezek. 20:6, 15; Dan. 11:16, 41). Again, we are told:

"He magnified himself . . . and by him the daily sacrifice was taken away" (Dan. 8:9-14).

According to the interpretation of Daniel's Vision, this Little Horn will be . . .

"a king of fierce countenance, and understanding dark sentences . . .
"his power shall be mighty, but not by his own power: and he shall destroy wonderfully, and shall prosper, and practice, and shall destroy the mighty and the holy people.
"And through his policy also he shall cause craft to prosper in his hand; and he shall magnify himself in his heart, and by peace shall destroy many: he shall also stand up against the Prince of princes; but he shall be broken without hand" (Dan. 8:23-25).

The Antichrist will not become prominent in world affairs until after the formation of the 10-nation confederacy. He will arise to power at the beginning of the Tribulation, and by the middle of the *"week"* (after three and one half years) he will be recognized as the beast of Revelation, Chapter 13.

The Antichrist will be a real person. He will have outstanding natural gifts and attract much interest and response. His power will come from Satan and his agents. The 10 kings will also give him their power and support.

Actually, Satan will give to the Antichrist that which he offered to Jesus Christ in Matthew 4:8; that is, the kingdoms of this world. Jesus, of course, refused the offer; but the Antichrist will accept it and then he will fight to keep it. He will pursue world conquest.

The 10 kings of the 10-nation confederacy . . .

"receive power as kings one hour with the beast. These have one mind, and shall give their power and strength unto the beast" (Rev. 17:12-13).

THE MAN OF SIN. Two errors had crept into the Church at Thessalonica, and both had reference to the Endtimes. The first had to do with the Rapture. The Apostle Paul had taught the Thessalonians that the Lord was soon to return and set up His Kingdom. Meanwhile some church members had died. Paul reassured the surviving members that death in no way negated the promise of the Rapture, the Second Coming, or the Millennium. All the Saints would participate in the Millennial Kingdom (I Thess. 4:13-18).

The second had to do with the Day of the Lord. Some church members thought they were already living in the Day of the Lord. Paul assured them that the Day of the Lord was a day of trouble and that that day would not come until the great apostasy or *"falling away"* had taken place and the *"man of sin"* was revealed. Paul went on to describe this Man of Sin. He is . . .

"the SON OF PERDITION;
"Who opposes and exalts himself above all that is called God, or that is worshipped; so that he as God sits in the Temple of God, showing himself that he is God . . .
"whose coming is after the working of Satan with all power and signs and lying wonders,
"And with all deceivableness of unrighteousness" (II Thess. 2:3-4, 9-10).

THE BEAST. The term *"beast"* is used several times in the Book of Revelation to refer to the Antichrist.

1. The first characteristic of the Beast is that he is different. He is so different that people will say:

"Who is like unto the beast?" (Rev. 13:4).

He is also described as *"diverse"* from all those kings who preceded him (Dan. 7:7, 19, 23-24). He will have all the world *"wondering"* after him (Rev. 13:3).

2. The second characteristic of the Beast is that he will possess an unusually high degree of intelligence. This Little Horn has . . .

"EYES LIKE THE EYES OF A MAN" (Dan. 7:8; Rev. 4:6)

... signifying intelligence. Satan will be so impressed by his unique abilities and qualifications for leadership that he will give him ...

"his power, and his seat, and great authority" (Rev. 13:2).

3. The third characteristic of the Beast is that he will have great powers of oratory. He will have ...

"a mouth speaking great things" (Dan. 7:8)

... indicating ability to command men. He will be able to sway the service of an able man to serve him as assistant (Rev. 13:11-17). His mouth is pictured as ...

"the mouth of a lion" (Rev. 13:2)

... indicating power and authority. Daniel saw him as a charismatic leader, a leader announcing peace, who would win the respect of the world through *"flatteries"* (Dan. 11:21, 32). The word *"flatteries"* meaning *"smooth slipperiness,"* and describes *"one who with smooth speech and seductive words or flattery attempts to win kingdoms."* However, blasphemy against God will be the chief characteristic of his speech (Rev. 13:1).

"There was given unto him a mouth speaking great things and blasphemies" (Rev. 13:5).

4. The fourth characteristic of the Beast is that he will be an astute politician.

"Through his policy also he shall cause craft to prosper in his hand" (Dan. 8:25).

He will see the value and influence of religion, and thereby submit himself, at least outwardly, to the false religious system (Rev. 17:3, 7). He will manipulate Israel into signing a seven-year covenant. He will not enter into this covenant for the sake of Israel, but to achieve his own diabolical ends. This will be evidenced when he breaks the covenant in the middle of the *"week"* (Dan. 9:27). At the same time he will turn on the religious system, the *"whore"* of Revelation 17:16-17. He will likewise persuade the 10 kings to surrender to his leadership their kingdoms (Rev. 17:12-13). Inevitably, they will follow the Antichrist into the Battle of Armageddon to their own destruction (Rev. 19:19-21).

5.   The fifth characteristic of the Beast is his strong physical appearance. He will be . . .

"a king of fierce countenance" (Dan. 8:23) . . .

"whose look was more stout than his fellows" (Dan. 7:20).

He will present a macho image that will command attention (II Thess. 2:4).

6.   The sixth characteristic of the Beast is his great military genius. His exploits will include the overthrow of three of the first kingdoms (Dan. 7:8, 24). He will go forth . . .

"conquering, and to conquer" (Rev. 6:1-2).

His military might will be convincing enough that his followers will say:

"Who is like unto the beast? Who is able to make war with him?" (Rev. 13:4).

7.   The seventh characteristic of the Beast is his religion and moral character. He will be the incarnation of sin, pride, arrogance, and unholy ambition. Some theologians believe the Prophecy that . . .

"in his estate shall he honour the god of forces" (Dan. 11:38)

. . . as indicating a revival of sorcery and witchcraft. Others see *"forces"* as *"fortresses,"* indicating that there will be safety and security in materialism. He also will have the capacity for . . .

"understanding dark sentences" (Dan. 8:23).

His unique powers will enable him to promote his claims of divinity (II Thess. 2:4). He will . . .

"exalt himself, and magnify himself above every god . . .

"Neither shall he regard the God of his fathers, nor the desire of women, nor regard any god: for he shall magnify himself above all" (Dan. 11:36-37).

Speaking of the coming Antichrist, Dave Hunt, in *Peace, Prosperity, and the Coming Holocaust,* wrote: *"When it came to swaying a huge audience, a nation, the world, no human was Hitler's equal. During his speeches, he was like a medium in a trance. Afterwards, like a medium who has been drained by the spirits, Hitler would collapse, deathly pale and exhausted. . . ."*

Hunt went on to quote the diary of Joseph Goebbels, who became Nazi Minister of Propaganda. In his diary, Goebbels revealed the hypnotic influence that Hitler exerted upon him when they first met: *"He is the creative instrument of fate and deity. I stand by him deeply shaken . . . recognize him as my leader . . . He is so deep and mystical . . . like a prophet of old."*

Many books have been written about Hitler's involvement in the occult, and we could make a good case that Hitler was controlled by Satan. And yet, be that as it may, Hitler will pale in the light of the coming Antichrist.

On September 30, 1939, Neville Chamberlain, British Prime Minister, returned from his conference in Munich, Germany, announcing, *"peace in our time,"* after he and Prime Minister Daladier of France had granted almost all of Hitler's demands that Czechoslovakia cede the Sudetenland to Germany.

Immediately Chamberlain became a hero. Six months later German tanks rolled across the almost defenseless Czechoslovakia.

Yes, Communists, like Chamberlain, believe in peace. Their idea of peace, however, is the time the last bourgeois (Capitalist) is exterminated and the so-called Proletariat (peasant) rules the world.

Daniel said of the coming Antichrist, the white horse rider of Revelation 6:2, that . . .

"He shall enter peaceably even upon the fattest places of the province" (Dan. 11:24).

A deceiver, he will claim to be the light of the world. His coming will be . . .

"with all power and signs and lying wonders,
"And with all deceivableness of unrighteousness in them who perish; because they received not the love of the Truth,

that they might be Saved" (II Thess. 2:9-10).

The Antichrist's great success will be his ability to convince the nations, like Chamberlain, that he will bring *"peace in our time."*

An editorial in a leading newspaper expressed the sentiment: *"In this holiest of seasons, the Mideast cries out for a Saviour to come forth — some great prophet or statesman who will break through the entanglements of violence, religious entities, and fears and inspire the people of the region with a vision of peace and brotherhood . . . a prophet statesman must step forward."*

The world is ripe for the rise of the Antichrist, who will promise peace, but we know that the world will not find rest and peace until the Prince of Peace ushers in the Millennial Kingdom.

THE BEGINNING OF SORROWS

We cannot really imagine the horrors of the future Tribulation. The Bible says:

> *"Then shall be GREAT TRIBULATION, such as was not since the beginning of the world to this time, no, nor ever shall be.*
> *"And except those days should be shortened, there should no flesh be saved"* (Mat. 24:21-22).

As terrible as were the events of World War II, with the Holocaust and the nuclear bombing of Hiroshima and Nagasaki . . . as terrible as was the *"purge"* under Russia's Stalin when an estimated 20 million lost their lives . . . as terrible as was the mass slaughters in Southeast Asia during the post-Vietnamese War era . . . they will be as nothing compared to the horrors of the Great Tribulation.

The white horse rider of Revelation 6:2 will be a deceiver. He will come in on a white horse, symbolic of purity and Messiahship. But with him will come war, famine, death, pestilence . . .

> *"and Hell followed with him"* (Rev. 6:8).

His coming will be . . .

> *"after the working of Satan with all power and signs and lying wonders,*
> *"And with all deceivableness of unrighteousness in them*

who perish; because they received not the love of the Truth, that they might be Saved.

"And for this cause God shall send them strong delusion, that they should believe a lie:

"That they all might be damned who believed not the Truth, but had pleasure in unrighteousness" (II Thess. 2:9-12).

Millions of people on this Earth will be fooled into thinking that the Man of Sin is really the Jews' Messiah.

The red horse rider of Revelation 6:4 comes with a great sword, with which to take peace from the Earth and to cause murder, war, and bloodshed. There can be no question about the symbolism here. War will be the natural result of the Antichrist going forth . . .

"conquering, and to conquer" (Rev. 6:2; cf. Dan. 7:24; 11:43-45; Mat. 24:6-7).

The red horse represents the military conquest of the Antichrist. He will plunge the Earth into a bloodbath of unprecedented proportions. His ultimate goal will be to conquer the world and to rule the world as a dictator. However, he will succeed only in overtaking the Old Roman Empire territory and its borders. His promise of peace will be just that — a promise. Peace will never come until the Prince of Peace returns to rule and reign over the world. The Bible forewarns us:

"You shall hear of wars and rumors of wars: see that you be not troubled: for all these things must come to pass, but the end is not yet" (Mat. 24:6).

The black horse rider of Revelation 6:5 has . . .

"a pair of balances in his hand."

This will be for the purpose of measuring food, indicating a severe scarcity (Ezek. 4:10-17). Famine is naturally a by-product of war because of a lack of men to till the soil and harvest the crops. During the Great Tribulation severe famine will grip parts of the world. Millions of people will starve, as food will not be grown in those areas where wars are being fought. This will be a time of great loss of life.

The pale horse rider of Revelation 6:8 brings death.

"And power was given unto them over the fourth part of

the Earth, to kill with sword, and with hunger, and with death, and with the beasts of the Earth" (Rev. 6:8).

The pronoun *"them"* indicates that there are actually two pale horse riders . . .

"Death, and Hell" (Rev. 6:8)

. . . since both are named and capitalized. Most of the people who die during this particular time will be lost and will go to Hell.

However, out of the Great Tribulation also will come the tribulation martyrs: those persons who . . .

"overcame him by the Blood of the Lamb, and by the word of their testimony; and they loved not their lives unto the death" (Rev. 12:11).

These Martyrs are not the Church, but those who will have been Saved after the Rapture of the Church. They will be killed because they will not serve the Antichrist or the world system. They will serve God, and war will be declared on them by the Antichrist. They literally will die by the thousands, tens of thousands, maybe even millions. Their only crime will be that they believed God and witnessed to His Goodness.

From underneath the Altar in Heaven these Martyrs will cry out:

"How long, O Lord, Holy and True, do you not judge and avenge our blood on them who dwell on the Earth?" (Rev. 6:10).

In the next Verse the Bible tells us that they will have to wait until all who will be slain during those years will be killed, and then they will be *"changed"* together at the end of the Great Tribulation.

SIGNS IN THE HEAVENS

Up to this point in the narrative, we have been reading how the Antichrist will bring pain and suffering upon the world. But with Revelation 6:12, we begin to read how God Himself will bring catastrophic destruction to this Planet.

This outpouring of God's Wrath will produce earthquakes. The sun will become black . . .

"as sackcloth of hair, and the moon . . . as blood" (Rev. 6:12).

There have been three times in history that the sun became black: (1) in the beginning (Gen. 1:2), (2) as a plague upon Egypt (Ex. 10:21-23), and (3) at the Crucifixion (Mat. 27:45). This may have occurred at other times, but not to the extent of these three occasions or to the extent that will take place in the Great Tribulation.

Actually five times during the Great Tribulation the moon will become as blood, and this will correspond to the darkening of the sun.

Next, we are told that the stars of Heaven will fall onto the Earth. Five times this will happen. These falling stars will be meteorites. When meteorites hit our atmosphere, they burn up. But occasionally they hit the Earth. The largest recorded meteorite weighed about 65,000 pounds (over 30 tons), but during the Tribulation there will be meteor showers where huge bodies will fly into the Earth with gigantic force and will be greater than an atomic explosion.

Jesus spoke of the day when the cry would go up to the mountains and hills:

> *"Then shall they begin to say to the mountains, Fall on us; and to the hills, Cover us"* (Lk. 23:30).

Natural hiding places, however, will be inadequate to shield anyone from God's Wrath.

> *"And the Heaven departed as a scroll when it is rolled together; and every mountain and island were moved out of their places"* (Rev. 6:14).

This does not mean that the Heavens cease to exist. It does mean that cataclysmic changes, through earthquakes, volcanoes, and natural and supernatural events that we cannot even imagine, will take place. The Earth and the Heavens will be altered by the Power of Almighty God.

> *"And the kings of the Earth, and the great men, and the rich men, and the chief captains, and the mighty men, and every bondman, and every free man, hid themselves in the dens and in the rocks of the mountains;*
> *"And said to the mountains and rocks, Fall on us, and hide us from the face of Him Who sits on the Throne, and from the Wrath of the Lamb:*
> *"For the great day of His Wrath is come; and who shall be able to stand?"* (Rev. 6:15-17).

MERCY IN THE MIDST OF WRATH

In the midst of wrath God remembers Mercy (cf. Hab. 3:2) and suspends Judgment. Judgment winds have been blowing, but now there is a lull in the storm. God stops the storm to show Mercy.

When God saves us, He does not change the world to suit us; rather He equips us to live in a world that is becoming increasingly worse. In wrath God remembered Mercy on the night of the Passover in Egypt (Ex. 11:4-7). In wrath God remembered Mercy before the Flood in Noah's day (Gen. 7:23). In wrath God remembered Mercy before the destruction of Sodom and Gomorrah, (Gen. 19:15-16). In wrath God remembered Mercy at Calvary (Jn. 3:16-17).

God's usual instrument for suspending Judgment is His Servants, the Angels. Here we read of four mighty Angels, standing on the four corners of the Earth, holding the four winds (that is, the four compass points — north, south, east, west).

In Elijah's day God reserved 7,000 in Israel who had not bowed to Baal (I Ki. 19:18). Likewise, God will have 144,000 Jews who will not bow to the Antichrist, but will accept the Lord Jesus Christ as Saviour. From each of the Twelve Tribes will come 12,000 Jews.

That these were not raptured reveals that they were not Born-Again until after the Rapture and the beginning of the Great Tribulation. They will be *"sealed"* or *"preserved, kept"* through the Judgments coming upon the Earth. Just as the Angel could not send Judgment on Sodom and Gomorrah until Lot had escaped (Gen. 19:22) . . . just as the Tribulation could not come until the Church had been raptured . . . so here the Angels cannot send Judgment until these 144,000 Jews are *"sealed."*

> *"Hurt not the Earth, neither the sea, nor the trees, till we have SEALED THE SERVANTS OF OUR GOD in their foreheads"* (Rev. 7:3).

This *"seal"* will be a literal, visible mark. The locusts of the abyss will be able to see it (Rev. 9:4). The seal of the Abrahamic Covenant was literal (Rom. 4:11). The sign of the Passover was literal (Ex. 12:13). The mark of the Beast will be literal (Rev. 13:16-18). This *"seal"* will be God's Name written in their forehead (Rev. 14:1).

At this time the Antichrist will be seeking world dominion and he will be angered, no doubt, by the sealing of the 144,000 Jews. Therefore, he will try to destroy them. Possibly from this, he will adopt the idea of sealing his own people.

Those who have the Seal of God in their forehead will be protected from the Wrath of God. Out of the Great Tribulation will come a great multitude of Saints . . .

" which no man could number, of all nations, and kindreds, and people, and tongues" (Rev. 7:9).

THE TEMPLE

Sometime during or just before the Great Tribulation, the Jews will rebuild their Temple. It is clear from both Testaments that during the Tribulation the old Jewish sacrificial form of worship will be reinstituted.

An article in the *Jerusalem Post* reveals *"the aspirations concerning the third Temple for whose speedy rebuilding Jews pray daily according to their traditional prayer book."*

During the Tribulation, the orthodox Jews will think their prayers have been answered when the Temple is reconstructed in its rightful place. However, midway in the *"week"* the Antichrist will desecrate the Temple with the . . .

"abomination that makes desolate" (Dan. 12:11).

This desecration of the Temple will continue for three and one half years.

SEVEN TRUMPET JUDGMENTS

After the sealing of the 144,000 Jews, the Angels will go forth to sound their trumpets, and with each trumpet blast will come a Divine Judgment, somewhat similar to the plagues of Egypt (cf. Ex. 7:19 through 10:29; 12:29-36), yet as we know, considerably worse.

1. FIRST TRUMPET JUDGMENT (Rev. 8:7) — hail, fire, and blood. The result of this Judgment will be that one-third of the trees and green grass will be destroyed.

2. SECOND TRUMPET JUDGMENT (Rev. 8:8-9) — a burning mountain. The result of this Judgment will be that one-third of the seas will be turned to blood, one-third of the sea creatures will die, and one-third of the ships will be destroyed.

3. THIRD TRUMPET JUDGMENT (Rev. 8:10-11) — the falling star. The result of this Judgment will be that one-third of the rivers and waters will be made bitter, and consequently many

SELF-HELP
STUDY NOTES

87

people will die.

4. FOURTH TRUMPET JUDGMENT (Rev. 8:12-13) — darkness. The result of this Judgment will be that one-third of the sun, moon, and stars will be darkened or prevented from shedding their light. Daylight and nighttime will be affected so that there will be one-third less illumination than there normally would be.

5. FIFTH TRUMPET JUDGMENT (Rev. 9:1-12) — opening of the bottomless pit. The result of this Judgment will be that demon locusts will be sent to hurt those who do not have the Seal of God in their forehead. Those affected will be tormented for five months. They will seek death, but will not find it. They will desire to die, but death will flee from them.

6. SIXTH TRUMPET JUDGMENT (Rev. 9:13-21) — invasion. As a result of this Judgment, armies will come against men and slay one-third of them.

7. SEVENTH TRUMPET JUDGMENT (Rev. 11:14-19) — Satan cast out of Heaven. The Devil himself will cause great havoc to the inhabitants of the Earth because he knows his time is short!

TWO WITNESSES

God loves the Jewish people, and in the midst of all this holocaust and destruction He will send two witnesses to testify to them of the Living God. They will prophesy for three and one half years . . .

"clothed in sackcloth" (Rev. 11:3).

It is stated that . . .

"These are the two olive trees, and the two candlesticks standing before the God of the Earth" (Rev. 11:4)

. . . which the Prophet Zechariah foretold (Zech. 4:1-14). These are identified as Enoch and Elijah, for they were both Prophets who were translated without tasting death (Zech. 4:11-14; Mal. 4:5; Heb. 9:27; Rev. 11:3-12).

They will be given power, or authority, and the right to exercise it as they choose. If any man tries to hurt them, fire will come out of their mouth to devour their enemies. They will have power to shut up the heavens, so that it will not rain during their Prophecy. They will have power to turn water to blood and to smite the Earth with all kinds of plagues as often as they will (Rev. 11:5-6).

Having completed their testimony, they will be at the mercy of their enemies. Whereas during their Prophecy they had the power and authority to devour their enemies, at the end of their Prophecy power will be given to the Beast, the Antichrist, to overcome them and to kill them.

Their dead bodies will lie in the street of the Holy City for three and one half days.

> *"And they of the people and kindreds and tongues and nations shall see their dead bodies . . . and shall not suffer their dead bodies to be put in graves"* (Rev. 11:9).

There will be gloating and merriment over the death of these two men of God — much as there was gloating and merriment over the death of men like Mussolini and Stalin . . .

> *"because these two Prophets tormented them who dwell on the Earth"* (Rev. 11:10).

After three and one half days the Spirit of God will enter into them, and they will stand on their feet. Naturally great fear will fall on all those watching. They will ascend into the clouds in the sight of their enemies. At the same time a great earthquake will shake the Holy City, and one-tenth of the city will be leveled and 7,000 people will die.

REVIVAL OF SORCERY

Nimrod, the mighty hunter, built the city of Babylon (Gen. 10:8-10), and it was here that the first great apostasy against God came after the Flood. Developed by Nimrod and his queen, Semiramis, the Babylonian cult concerned the divination of secrets and mysteries in various priestly functions — esoteric knowledge and occultism.

Under Nimrod this cult gained an influential stronghold on the human race. It counteracted the Truth of God, and as it spread and developed more fully, the city of Babylon came to be known as the seat of Satan or Satan worship.

The terms *"the great whore"* and *"the woman"* are sometimes used in Scripture in connection with idolatrous Israel, Babylon, and other pagan nations (Isa. 13:8; 54:6; Jer. 3:9; 4:31; 6:2, 24; 31:27; Lam. 1:17; Ezek. 16:17-36; 20:30; 23:3-44; 43:7-9; Hos. 4:10-12). These terms never are used of professing Christians in any respect.

The religion of Babylon (the city is mentioned six times in the Book of Revelation) in the Last Days can best be described as relating to witchcraft, demon worship, and manifestations of demons (Rev. 9:20-21; 13:2; Dan. 11:37-38; Mat. 24:24; II Thess. 2:8-12). The religion of Mystery Babylon will be anti-God — completely and totally. It involves ancient magic, spiritism, sorcery, idolatry, and paganism.

There is a revival today in the area of witchcraft, astrology, black arts, and black magic. There are even circles where human sacrifices are being offered. The world is ripe for a religion in which demon spirits are active.

While the city of Babylon will be rebuilt in the Last Days, Mystery Babylon is not a city, but a mystery religion; that is, the occult. This religion will ride the Beast and assist him in his rise to power. The Antichrist will establish this as a state religion, and all who do not follow him in worship will be martyred.

A CALL TO SEPARATION

"And I heard another voice from Heaven, saying, Come out of her, My People, that you be not partakers of her sins, and that you receive not of her plagues.

"For her sins have reached unto Heaven, and God has remembered her iniquities.

"Reward her even as she rewarded you, and double unto her according to her works: in the cup which she has filled, fill to her double.

"How much she has glorified herself, and lived deliciously, so much torment and sorrow give her: for she said in her heart, I sit a queen, and am no widow, and shall see no sorrow.

"Therefore shall her plagues come in one day, death, and mourning, and famine; and she shall be utterly burned with fire: for strong is the Lord God Who judges her" (Rev. 18:4-8).

Here we see a clear call to separation. God's People in any age are called out, to leave the company of evildoers, to separate themselves from the place of iniquity. Mystery Babylon and her worshippers will be judged and punished. If anyone desires not to partake of her punishment, then he must separate himself, so as not to partake of her sins.

Many well-meaning people have thought they could remain within an apostate religious system in an effort to reform it or not to offend it. But God's Command is clear:

"And what concord has Christ with Belial? or what part

has he who believes with an infidel?

"And what agreement has the Temple of God with idols? for you are the Temple of the Living God . . .

"WHEREFORE COME OUT FROM AMONG THEM, AND BE YE SEPARATE, SAITH THE LORD, and touch not the unclean thing; and I will receive you" (II Cor. 6:15-17).

God has always called His People to separation. The call came to Abraham (Gen. 12:1), to Moses (Num. 16:23-26), to Israel (Isa. 48:20; Jer. 50:8; 51:6, 45).

Today we are seeing many Hollywood celebrities and sports celebrities and other celebrities who are *professing* Christians. Yet it seems they never leave the world. This is not God's Way. God has called His People to be *in* the world, but not *of* the world (Jn. 17:14-16). When *professing* Saints go into nightclubs and other dark places of this world to perform and supposedly give a silent witness, they are in fact violating God's Law of separation. Inevitably instead of them rubbing off on the world, the world rubs off on them.

Just as God wanted Lot out of Sodom, so He wants His People out of today's *"Sodom and Gomorrahs,"* which are standing under the Wrath of God. Someday God will destroy Mystery Babylon.

"She shall be UTTERLY BURNED WITH FIRE" (Rev. 18:8).

The line of separation will be drawn as the kings of the Earth and the merchants who trafficked with her . . .

"shall bewail her, and lament for her" (Rev. 18:9) . . .

"shall weep and mourn over her" (Rev. 18:11)

. . . while the people of God shall rejoice over her (Rev. 18:20).

SEVEN VIALS OF WRATH

In addition to the Seven Trumpet Judgments, there will be what is called the seven last plagues, filled with the Wrath of God. These seven plagues are contained in seven golden Vials, which will be poured out upon the Earth (see Rev., Chpt. 15).

1. FIRST VIAL (Rev. 16:2) — sores. The Bible refers to these sores as *"noisome,"* from the Greek *kakos,* meaning *"depraved"* or *"injurious."* The sores are also called *"grievous,"* from the

Greek *poneros,* meaning *"culpable," "diseased," "atrociously wicked,"* and *"malignant."* These sores will come . . .

"upon the men which had the mark of the beast, and upon them which worshipped his image."

2. SECOND VIAL (Rev. 16:3) — sea turned to blood. When the second Angel pours out his Vial upon the sea, it will become . . .

"as the blood of a dead man"

. . . and every living soul in the sea will die.

3. THIRD VIAL (Rev. 16:4-7) — water turned to blood. This plague is like the second, except it concerns rivers and fountains of waters. The reason for this kind of plague is attributed to the fact that the Beast and those of his kingdom . . .

"have shed the blood of Saints and Prophets."

And now they will have blood to drink. This shows the exactness of God's Justice (Rev. 16:7).

4. FOURTH VIAL (Rev. 16:8-9) — scorching heat. When the Angel pours out the fourth plague, the power of the sun will be unleashed upon men, so that it will scorch men with fire and great heat. Instead of turning men to God, this plague, as others, only will harden their heart and they will blaspheme the Name of God . . .

"which has power over these plagues: and THEY RE-PENTED NOT to give Him Glory."

The attitude of these men closely parallels the attitude of Pharaoh when the plagues were poured out on Egypt (Ex., Chpts. 7 through 12).

5. FIFTH VIAL (Rev. 16:10-11) — darkness. When the fifth Angel pours out his Vial, the kingdom of the Beast will be filled with dense darkness, and men will gnaw their tongue for pain and blaspheme God because of their sores, and still not repent of their evil deeds. The word *"darkness"* here is the Greek *skotos,* meaning *"obscurity"* or *"shadiness."*

6. SIXTH VIAL (Rev. 16:12) — Euphrates River dried up. The

purpose of this is stated:

"That the way of the kings of the east might be prepared."

7. SEVENTH VIAL (Rev. 16:17-21) — earthquake and hail. At the outpouring of the seventh Vial, there will be an earthquake unparalleled in the history of the Earth.

"There was a great earthquake, such as was not since men were upon the Earth, so mighty an earthquake, and so great."

As the result of the quake whole cities will be leveled. Mountains and islands will be moved out of their place. Also, hail the weight of a talent (*c.* 110 pounds) will rain upon the Earth. Still men will not repent, but blaspheme God.

MARK OF THE BEAST

When the Beast comes into full power and authority, he will be able to exercise all the power of a full-fledged dictator, and even more, all the power of a sorcerer or medium. He will make many demands of the people. He will command their allegiance, their worship, and, in effect, their livelihood. He will exercise total control of those whom he governs.

At some point in the Tribulation, probably midway, he will require all his subjects to receive a mark in their right hand or in their forehead in order to buy or sell (Rev. 13:16-18). Some people, of course, will refuse, and for this they will be executed (Rev. 7:9-17; 13:7; 14:13; 15:2-3; 20:4).

In a way that we do not fully understand, this mark will be tied in with occult worship, so that in taking the mark a person commits apostasy, and can never be Saved. To take the mark the individual must totally deny Jesus Christ and, in so many words, sell his soul to the Devil.

There are three features of this adherence to the Beast:

1. MARK OF THE BEAST. This is different from the name of the Beast or the number of his name. We do not know what the mark will be, but it must be an emblem, like a tattoo or laser image, imprinted on or under the skin that stands for the kingdom of the Antichrist (Rev. 13:16).

2. NAME OF THE BEAST. We do not know the name of the Beast, but during the Tribulation, of course, he will ultimately be identified. Instead of receiving a mark, a person may receive his name. Like the mark it may be tattooed or imprinted on the body (Rev. 13:17).

3. NUMBER OF THE BEAST. Revelation 13:17 says *"number of his name,"* and Revelation 13:18 says *"number of the beast."* Like the emblem and the name, it must be an ID number that can be tattooed or imprinted on the right hand or forehead. His number is 666.

Many people have tried to calculate the number of the Beast. Someone has said it refers to the Latin Kingdom (Romanism), which has been tallied to 666. Others have said the Greek letters of the alphabet have numerical meaning, and as such may be tallied to a sum total. We do not really know at this point in time what the number of the Beast means, even though we are told it is 666. Someday this information will prove useful to those left behind to go through the Great Tribulation. God has given us this information for our profit, and there is no doubt that it will be significantly useful someday.

> *"Here is wisdom. Let him who has understanding count the number of the beast: for it is the number of a man; and his number is Six hundred threescore and six"* (Rev. 13:18).

MAN CHILD

Besides the Antichrist, the two witnesses, and the 144,000 Jews, several other *"actors"* have a part in the unfolding drama of the Great Tribulation.

> *"And she brought forth a manchild, who was to rule all nations with a rod of iron: and her child was caught up unto God, and to His Throne"* (Rev. 12:5).

There are several theories concerning the Man Child. Some persons teach that the Man Child is Christ, and for this they give the following reasons:

1. The Man Child came from Israel *"concerning the flesh"* (Rom. 9:4-5). However, as we know, *any son of Israel* could be taken as the Man Child.

2. The Man Child is to rule the nations *"with a rod of iron"* (Rev. 19:15; Ps. 2:9). This expression means authority over the nations. All of the Redeemed and resurrected Saints will have authority in Christ. The Old Testament Saints will reign with Christ (Ps. 149:6-9; Dan. 7:18; Mat. 8:11-12). The Church will rule with

Christ (Mat. 19:28; 20:20-28; Rom. 8:17; I Cor. 4:8; 6:2; II Tim. 2:12; Rev. 1:5-6; 2:26-27). The 144,000 Jews will reign with Christ (Rev. 7:1-8; 12:5; 14:1-5). The Tribulation Saints and Martyrs will reign with Christ (Rev. 20:4-6). So, we see that all Saints from all ages will rule with Christ, and we could conclude that the phrase *"with a rod of iron"* could as easily apply to them.

3. The Man Child was caught up to God's Throne (cf. Eph. 1:20). Again, this is not conclusive proof that Christ is the Man Child. John had witnessed the historical Ascension of Christ over 60 years prior to the Revelation, and he made no connection between the two events.

4. The Man Child is called a *"man"* (cf. I Tim. 2:5). It is true that Christ is sometimes referred to as *"The Man,"* but this is insufficient evidence, as others are also called a *"man"* in Scripture.

Other persons teach that the Man Child is the Church. Another teaching is that the Man Child represents the Bride of Christ. Still another teaching is that the Man Child represents only those who are baptized in the Holy Spirit. The Parable of the Ten Virgins (Mat. 25:1-13) is given as Scriptural support for this theory.

We believe the true interpretation is that the Man Child symbolizes the 144,000 Jews. When the Man Child is brought forth, the dragon will try to devour him as soon as he is born, but the Man Child will be . . .

"caught up unto God, and to His Throne" (Rev. 12:5).

This means the Man Child will be a *living* company, because dead or resurrected people would not be subject to the threat of the dragon. The one remaining company of the redeemed, and the only one altogether composed of living Saints, will be the 144,000 Jews who will be sealed during the Trumpet Judgments.

Since the 144,000 Jews are seen in Heaven during the last half of the Tribulation, they evidently will be *"caught up"* in the middle of it (Rev. 14:1-5). God will protect the Man Child from the dragon and the Antichrist.

This company of the 144,000 Jews will appear before the Throne in Heaven and . . .

"before the four Beasts, and the Elders" (Rev. 14:3).

. . . who are before the Throne. The statement is made that they are . . .

95

"redeemed from the Earth" (Rev. 14:3) . . .

"redeemed from among men" (Rev. 14:4).

The privileges of the 144,000 Jews show them to be a special company. They are from the Earth, they have been redeemed, and they are a part of the First Resurrection. They will form one of the wondrous choirs of Heaven and sing a secret song that no one knows but themselves. Others will understand the words, but they will not have the particular experience that is described. It will be a new song, sung by a new company, with a new theme, giving credence to the thought that they will be that *living* company saved from the dragon and saved out of Great Tribulation.

That they will not be . . .

"defiled with women; for they are virgins" (Rev. 14:4)

. . . indicates that they will have abstained from the fornication of Mystery Babylon.

SUN-CLOTHED WOMAN

Unless we are told otherwise, we should take the Book of Revelation literally; that is, if it says *"woman,"* it means a woman; if it says *"star,"* it means a star; if it says *"mountain,"* it means a mountain. However, the depiction of the sun-clothed woman is not to be taken literally. The Apostle John, in his writing, said it was a *"wonder"* (Rev. 12:1) or *"sign."* The Greek word for *"wonder"* used here is *semeion,* meaning *"sign"* or *"symbol."*

Who is the sun-clothed woman?

Some persons believe the woman refers to the Virgin Mary giving birth to the blessed Saviour. If the Apostle John thought this was the meaning, no doubt he would have said so.

Other persons think the woman refers to the Holy City, Jerusalem. However, it is contrary to the nature of things for a material earthly city to take wings and fly away to the wilderness, and after 1,260 days to return.

Still other persons think the woman refers to the Church. However, this is inconsistent with God's dealing exclusively with Israel during this period of events.

We believe the woman symbolizes the Nation of Israel; that is, all the Jews who will be in Palestine during the 70th *"week"* of Daniel's Prophetic time line (Dan. 9:24-27). There are several reasons for accepting this interpretation.

1. Israel is often mentioned in Scripture as a married woman (Isa. 54:1-6; Jer. 3:1-14). The Book of Hosea presents the idea of Israel being married to God and pictures her backslidings and immorality as infidelity. After her subsequent humiliation and brokenness in the wilderness, she returns to her husband, God (Hos. 2:14-23; Rom., Chpt., 11; Acts 15:13-18).

2. Three classes of people are recognized in the Bible: (1) the Jews, (2) the Gentiles, (3) the Church. During the Tribulation the Church will have been raptured, leaving only the Jews and the Gentiles. The sun-clothed woman would not be the Gentiles or the Jews of the Diaspora. Consequently, she must be the Jews who have come out of the nations and returned to the Promised Land. After Revelation, Chapter 4 there is no reference to the Church on Earth; there is reference only to the Jews.

3. The woman . . .

"being with child cried, travailing in birth, and pained to be delivered" (Rev. 12:2).

The word *"pained"* is the Greek *basanizo* and means *"torment"* and *"torture."* The same word is used in Revelation 9:5; 11:10; 14:10; and 20:10. Israel will suffer pain, torment, and torture during the Tribulation Period, also called . . .

"the time of Jacob's trouble" (Jer. 30:7).

In her past history Israel has been in bondage many times, beginning with the Children of Israel in Egypt (Ex. 1:7-14; 2:23-25) and culminating with the Holocaust in Europe in World War II. There is no denying that Israel has experienced pain.

However, this travail and tribulation will be the worst she has ever known.

"There shall be A TIME OF TROUBLE, such as never was since there was a nation even to that same time" (Dan. 12:1).

"Then shall be GREAT TRIBULATION, such as was not since the beginning of the world to this time, no, nor ever shall be" (Mat. 24:21).

THE SATANIC TRINITY

"And there appeared another wonder in Heaven; and

behold a great red dragon . . .

"and the dragon stood before the woman which was ready to be delivered, for to devour her child as soon as it was born" (Rev. 12:3-4).

For over 1,900 years the Jews have wandered over the Earth being cursed, spat upon, stoned, and killed as a result of persecution.

In 1897 Theodor Herzl, a journalist, called for the first Zionist World Congress to meet in Switzerland, to organize a worldwide movement for the return of the Jews to their Land — the rebirth of a free and independent Israel.

In 1903, a great massacre of Jews launched in Russia backfired and resulted in 30,000 Russian and Polish Jews returning to Palestine. Among these was the first Prime Minister, David Ben-Gurion.

Later, Chaim Weizmann, a Russian Jew and a scientist living in England at the time of World War I, was to be honored by the King of England, George V, for his scientific discovery of a chemical vital to the British military. He made a request of the king: *"I want nothing for myself. All I desire is a Homeland for my people."* This resulted in England establishing a Homeland in Palestine for the Jews. Consequently, Jews from all over the world began pouring into Palestine.

Obviously, this was a threat to the Arabs, and so the dragon stirred up the Arabs to object to Jewish immigration. Because of England's vast oil interests in the Middle East, she yielded to the Arab demands and restricted Jewish immigration and purchases of all real estate.

In 1939 England issued what was known as the white paper, limiting Jewish immigration to 15,000 a year for five years. This became a death warrant to the Jews. It closed the door for thousands and thousands of Jews trying to escape Hitler's death camps.

After World War II Jews in Palestine numbered about a half million, and were the target of about one million Palestinian Arabs. The next few years were years of terror for the surviving Jews. The dragon was determined to exterminate the Jews and to confiscate their land. During the next few years, the world's conscience was awakened to the devastation of the Jews in Hitler's crematoriums. As a result, the United Nations carved out a Homeland for the Jews in Palestine, which was to go into effect May 4, 1948.

On that date the combined armies of Lebanon, Syria, Jordan, Iraq, and Egypt moved in for what they called a war of extermination and a massacre. Again, the dragon was trying to destroy God's chosen People, the Nation of Israel. But when the smoke of war settled, Israel was victor.

This has been the story of the Jews. Satan — the dragon — has been unrelenting in his effort to destroy them, as can be seen by the three major wars that were to follow (in 1956, in 1967, and in 1973). Why? Because Israel was chosen by God to bring about His Plan for the Redemption of the world.

The dragon of Revelation is certainly an appropriate symbol for Satan. Jesus said:

> *"The thief comes not, but for to steal, and to kill, and to destroy"* (Jn. 10:10).

Satan is portrayed in Scripture as . . .

> *"Leviathan"* (Job 41:1-34) . . .

> *"Leviathan the piercing serpent"* (Isa. 27:1) . . .

> *"Leviathan that crooked serpent"* (Isa. 27:1) . . .

> *"The great dragon . . . that old serpent, called the Devil, and Satan, which deceives the whole world"* (Rev. 12:9) . . .

> *"The dragon, that old serpent, which is the Devil, and Satan"* (Rev. 20:2).

Just as there is a Heavenly Trinity (God the Father, God the Son, and God the Holy Spirit), there will be a Satanic trinity (the Devil, the Antichrist, and the False Prophet). Just as Jesus Christ was filled with the Spirit of God and did the Will of the Father and had Power with God, so the Antichrist of the Great Tribulation will be possessed of the Devil and do the will of his father (cf. Jn. 8:44) and have supernatural power from the pit.

> *"And the beast which I saw was like unto a leopard, and his feet were as the feet of a bear, and his mouth as the mouth of a lion: and THE DRAGON GAVE HIM HIS POWER, AND HIS SEAT, AND GREAT AUTHORITY.*
> *"And they worshipped the dragon which gave power unto the beast"* (Rev. 13:2, 4).

In addition to the Dragon, and the Beast (the Antichrist), there appears in the Book of Revelation *"another beast"* called the False Prophet.

> *"And I beheld ANOTHER BEAST coming up out of the Earth; and he had two horns like a lamb, and he spoke as a*

99

DRAGON" (Rev. 13:11).

The False Prophet shall promote the Beast (the Antichrist) and force the people to give their allegiance and worship unto this man. The False Prophet . . .

> *"exercises all the power of the first beast before him, and causes the Earth and them who dwell therein to worship the first beast . . .*
> *"And he does great wonders, so that he makes fire come down from Heaven on the Earth in the sight of men,*
> *"And deceives them who dwell on the Earth by the means of those miracles which he had power to do in the sight of the beast"* (Rev. 13:12-14).

It is the False Prophet who will *"market"* the Beast and coerce worship to his image. It is the False Prophet who will cause all people to receive the mark of the Beast in order to buy or sell.

At the time of the end . . .

> *"three unclean spirits like frogs come out of the mouth of the DRAGON, and out of the mouth of the BEAST, and out of the mouth of the FALSE PROPHET"* (Rev. 16:13)

. . . to lure the kings of the Earth to the Battle of Armageddon.

Ultimately the Devil, the Beast, and the False Prophet will share the same fate.

> *"And the BEAST was taken, and with him the FALSE PROPHET . . . These both were cast alive into a Lake of Fire burning with brimstone"* (Rev. 19:20).

> *"And the DEVIL . . . was cast into the Lake of Fire and brimstone, where the BEAST and the FALSE PROPHET are"* (Rev. 20:10).

JUDGMENT SEAT OF CHRIST

During this seven-year period of time, referred to as Daniel's 70th *"week"* and the Tribulation, the Church will appear before the Judgment Seat of Christ. This is sometimes called the Judgment of Works.

The Apostle Paul wrote that all of our Ministry, our labors in the harvest, our *"good works"* will be examined:

*"EVERY MAN'S WORK SHALL BE MADE MANIFEST . . .
because it shall be revealed by fire; and the fire shall try every
man's work of what sort it is.*

*"If any man's work abide which he has built thereupon, he
shall receive a reward"* (I Cor. 3:11-15).

He added later:

"Wherefore we labour, that . . . we may be accepted of Him.

*"For we must all appear before the JUDGMENT SEAT
OF CHRIST; that every one may receive the things done in his
body, according to that he has done"* (II Cor. 5:9-10).

The Bible refers to the Judgment Seat of Christ as a recompense . . .

"at the resurrection of the just" (Lk. 14:14)

. . . showing it to be a separate occasion from the Great White Throne
Judgment (Rev. 20:11-15). Jesus spoke of rewards for the Righteous
(Mat. 5:11-12; 6:4, 18; 10:41-42), as did the Apostle Paul (I Cor. 9:17-
18; I Tim. 5:18).

*"For the Son of Man shall come . . . and then He shall
reward every man according to his works"* (Mat.16:27).

*"Behold, I come quickly; and My reward is with Me, to
give every man according as his work shall be"* (Rev. 22:12).

MARRIAGE SUPPER OF THE LAMB

Also, during this seven-year period of time, referred to as Daniel's
70th *"week"* and the Tribulation, the Church will be seated in Heaven at
the Marriage Supper of the Lamb (Rev. 19:7-9).

*"Let us be glad and rejoice, and give honour to Him: for
the MARRIAGE OF THE LAMB IS COME, and His Wife has
made herself ready.*

*"And to her was granted that she should be arrayed in fine
linen, clean and white: for the fine linen is the Righteousness
of Saints.*

*"And he said unto me, Write, BLESSED ARE THEY
WHICH ARE CALLED UNTO THE MARRIAGE SUPPER
OF THE LAMB"* (Rev. 19:7-9).

This is the only reference in the entire Bible to this glorious event, which will occur toward the end of the Great Tribulation when God will resurrect the Saints who have been martyred (Rev. 7:9-17) during this time. They will join with us as we sit down together at the Master's Table!

There is no description given of the wedding supper. The Greek word for *"marriage"* means *"marriage feast."* So no doubt this will be an actual literal supper just as we would enjoy here on Earth (cf. Mat. 22:2; 25:10).

At the time of Christ, a wife was almost always chosen for a man by his father (or near kinsman). A friend sometimes did the whole business of selecting the bride for the bridegroom. The espousal was legal and binding. Some time (usually one year) would pass between the espousal and the wedding. The bridegroom wore new clothes and a crown of gold. The wedding garment of the well-to-do bride was a display of fine clothing and jewels. Both parties perfumed themselves and made themselves *"ready."* The bride took a bath, attired herself in her fine garments, and put on her head a crown of jewels. Her shoes were given to her by the bridegroom. Then a procession, with music and singing, everyone carrying a lantern, escorted her to the house of the bridegroom, where the marriage supper was held. The wealthy prolonged the feast for days and furnished garments for the wedding guests.

> *"And I heard as it were the voice of a great multitude . . . saying . . . Let us be glad and rejoice, and give honour to Him: for THE MARRIAGE OF THE LAMB IS COME, AND HIS WIFE HAS MADE HERSELF READY"* (Rev. 19:6-7).

It is difficult to envision untold thousands of people participating in such an event, but nothing is impossible with God. When Christ meets the Saints in the air, He will take them to Heaven and present them to the Father (Jn. 14:1-3; I Thess. 3:13). The supper will take place just prior to the Second Coming when Christ will come from Heaven with His Saints (Zech. 14:5; Jude, Vss. 14-15; Rev. 19:11-21). When they leave Heaven to come back to Earth, they will come directly to Earth and deliver Israel and set up a New kingdom, which will never pass away!

Chapter 3

The Battle Of Armageddon

CHAPTER THREE

THE BATTLE OF ARMAGEDDON

The word *"Armageddon"* appears only once in Scripture; that is, Revelation 16:16.

> *"And He gathered them together into a place called in the Hebrew tongue ARMAGEDDON."*

"Armageddon" is derived from two Hebrew words: *har,* meaning *"a mountain or range of hills, or hill country,"* and *Megiddo,* meaning *"rendezvous."* The compound word refers to the Hill of Megiddo, which is on the south side of the Valley of Megiddo, or Esdraelon (II Chron. 35:22; Zech. 12:11), and southeast of Mount Carmel. Megiddo was the capital of a portion of the Land of Canaan that was given to Joshua (Josh. 12:21; 17:11; Judg. 1:27). It is located at the entrance to a pass across the Carmel Mountains, on the main route between Africa and Asia, and is the key position between the Euphrates River and the Nile River. Because of its strategic location, it has been the scene of many battles over the years. Thothmes III, founder of the Old Egyptian Empire, said, *"Megiddo is worth a thousand cities."*

The name *"Armageddon"* is becoming more and more prominent in newscasts and world focus. The late General Douglas MacArthur said that the next great conflict might well prove to be Armageddon. Of course, he meant *"Armageddon"* as a figure of speech, a metaphor. He was implying that modern weaponry had reached such a destructive level that it could well spell the end of the human race; that is, if all-out war were to lead to use of nuclear weapons.

Matthew, Chapter 24 intimates that the Great Tribulation and the Battle of Armageddon will be unparalleled in the history of mankind. If we pause to review history and think of Attila the Hun, Genghis Khan, Adolf Hitler, Joseph Stalin, and all the other despots of the ages, it is hard to comprehend that coming events could be worse, but worse they *will be*. The words of our Lord confirmed this, and so we can be sure that the Battle of Armageddon will be horrible indeed.

Some persons have speculated whether or not the United States of America will be involved in the Great Tribulation or the Battle of Armageddon. If we remember that the Bible is basically a Jewish Book, then we realize that God addresses other nations only as they relate to Israel.

Israel sprang from the loins of Abraham (see Gen., Chpts. 12; 15; 18).

Through Israel came the Branch, the Son of David, the Messiah, the Lord Jesus Christ — and yet they rejected Him. Consequently, their Holy City was leveled, and their people were scattered over the face of the Earth. The Jews have wandered for many years. And they have suffered. Oh, how they have suffered! Names like Dachau, Buchenwald, Treblinka, and Auschwitz stand as monuments of shame to a world gone mad under Adolf Hitler as some six million Jews were slaughtered during the Holocaust. The awful words of the Jews have reverberated down through the centuries:

"His Blood be on us, and on our children" (Mat. 27:25).

Oh, how these words have come to pass! So much so that this people long ago would have been exterminated if it were not for the restraining hand of Providence.

But they are coming home. There may be dark days ahead, but they are coming home. Despite its severity, the Great Tribulation (including the Battle of Armageddon) basically will have two purposes: (1) for God to pour out His Judgment on a world that has forgotten Him days without number (Jer. 2:32) and (2) to bring His chosen People, the Jews, back to Him.

Jesus prophesied that Israel would not accept Him as their Messiah, but another they would receive (Jn. 5:43). That other will be the Antichrist. It is a sad commentary on Israel that in the midst of her Great Tribulation she will think she has found her saviour — the Antichrist!

TIME OF THE BATTLE

Revelation, Chapter 16 places the Battle of Armageddon between the Sixth and Seventh Vials. At the Sixth Vial the Euphrates River will be dried up; at the Seventh Vial a great earthquake will take place and great hailstones will fall. Of course, we recognize the Seventh Vial as the description of Christ's Return in Zechariah 14:4-5. Therefore, we conclude that the Battle of Armageddon will occur at the time of the following:

1. WHEN THE ANTICHRIST CONQUERS RUSSIA, GERMANY, AND OTHER COUNTRIES ON THE PERIPHERY OF THE 10 KINGDOMS AND HAS MOBILIZED THE NATIONS AGAINST ISRAEL (Rev. 16:19-21; Dan. 11:44; Ezek., Chpts. 38-39; Zech. 14:1-5);

2. WHEN CHRIST RETURNS TO DELIVER ISRAEL FROM THE ANTICHRIST (Rev. 16:11-21; Joel, Chpt. 3; Zech. 14:1-5;

Isa. 63:1-7; Jude, Vs. 14; II Thess. 1:7);

3. AFTER THE GREAT TRIBULATION (Rev. 16:11-21; Mat. 24:29-31; 25:31-46);

4. AFTER THE MARRIAGE SUPPER OF THE LAMB (Rev. 19:1-21);

5. WHEN JERUSALEM IS SURROUNDED BY ARMIES (Rev. 16:19-21; Zech. 14:1-5);

6. JUST BEFORE THE MILLENNIUM (Rev. 16:11-21; 20:1-10);

7. AT THE END OF THE AGE (Rev. 16:11-21; Mat. 13:40-50; 24:29-31; 25:31-46; Acts 15:13-18);

8. WHEN GOD SETS UP HIS KINGDOM (Rev. 11:15; 17:14; 19:11-21; Dan. 2:44-45; 7:13-14, 18-27);

9. AFTER THE FIRST RESURRECTION (Rev. 16:19 through 20:6);

10. AT THE END OF DANIEL'S 70TH WEEK (Rev. 11:1-3; 12:6, 14; 13:5; Dan. 9:27);

11. AT THE DAY OF THE LORD (Rev. 19:11 through 20:7; I Thess. 5:3; II Thess., Chpt. 2);

12. AFTER THE ANTICHRIST HAS REIGNED THREE AND ONE HALF YEARS (Rev. 13:5; 19:19-21; II Thess. 2:8-9);

13. WHEN THE TARES AND WHEAT ARE SEPARATED (Mat. 13:40-50; 25:31-46);

14. WHEN CONDITIONS ARE LIKE THOSE OF THE DAYS OF NOAH AND LOT (Rev. 19:11-21; Mat. 24:37-39; Lk. 17:22-37; I Tim., Chpt. 4; II Tim. 3:1-13; 4:1-4; II Pet., Chpt. 2);

15. WHEN ISRAEL IS GATHERED FROM ALL NATIONS (Mat. 24:29-31; Isa. 11:10-12; Ezek., Chpt. 37);

16. JUST BEFORE SATAN IS BOUND (Rev. 19:11 through 20:7; Isa. 24:22, 23; 25:7);

17. WHEN THE TWO WITNESSES HAVE BEEN RESURRECTED AND HAVE ASCENDED (Rev. 11:3-14);

18. WHEN ISRAEL HAS BEEN IN THE WILDERNESS THREE AND ONE HALF YEARS (Rev. 11:1-3; 12:6, 14; 13:5);

19. WHEN THE SEALS, TRUMPETS, AND VIALS HAVE BEEN FULFILLED (Rev. 16:17-21; 19:1-21); AND,

20. ONE THOUSAND YEARS BEFORE THE NEW HEAVEN AND THE NEW EARTH (Rev. 19:11 through 20:10; 21:1).

DESCRIPTION OF THE BATTLE

The Second Coming of Christ and the Battle of Armageddon will take place the same day. The Bible refers to this day as *"the Day of the Lord."* This day will be a day of destruction and horrible devastation for the enemies of Israel and the Satanic alliance under the Antichrist. But, we must remember, it will be a wonderful, glorious day for Israel, whom the King will come to defend and rescue, and for the world, really, because it will be a grand and beautiful day of deliverance.

The expression *"Day of the Lord"* or *"that day"* is common to the Prophet Joel, although it is mentioned in other places in Scripture. *"The Day of the Lord"* will be . . .

1. A DAY OF DESTRUCTION (Joel 1:15);

2. A DAY OF DARKNESS (Joel 2:2; 3:15; Mat. 24:29-31);

3. A DAY OF GLOOM (Joel 2:2);

4. A DAY OF CLOUDS (Joel 2:2);

5. A DAY OF INVASION BY ALIEN FORCES (Joel 2:2-11);

6. A DAY OF FIRE (Joel 2:3);

7. A DAY OF PAIN (Joel 2:6);

8. A DAY OF GREAT TERROR (Joel 2:11, 31);

9. A DAY OF WAR (Joel 2:1; 3:9-16);

10. A DAY OF JUDGMENT (Joel 3:11-12; Mat. 25:31-46));

11. A DAY OF DECISION (Joel 3:14-16; Rev. 11:15);

12. A DAY OF EARTHQUAKES (Joel 3:16; Zech. 14:4-5; Rev. 16:17-21);

13. A DAY OF PREY (Zeph. 3:8; Isa. 34:6; Rev. 19:17-18);

14. A DAY OF DESOLATION (Zeph. 1:15);

15. A DAY OF THE LORD'S SACRIFICE (Zeph. 1:8);

16. A GREAT DAY OF THE LORD (Zeph. 1:14);

17. A DAY OF WRATH (Zeph. 1:15);

18. A DAY OF TROUBLE (Zeph. 1:15);

19. A DAY OF DISTRESS (Zeph. 1:15);

20. A DAY OF THE TRUMPET (Zeph. 1:16);

21. A DAY OF ALARM (Zeph. 1:16);

22. A DAY OF BLOODSHED (Zeph. 1:17; Rev. 14:20);

23. A DAY OF DEATH (Zeph. 1:18);

24. A DAY OF NOISE (Zeph. 1:10);

25. A DAY OF BITTER CRYING (Zeph. 1:14);

26. A DAY OF PUNISHMENT (Zeph. 1:8-9, 12);

27. A DAY OF SLAUGHTER (Isa. 34:2);

28. A DAY OF PESTILENCE (Ezek. 38:22);

29. A DAY OF HAIL (Ezek. 38:22; Rev. 16:21); AND,

30. A DAY OF THUNDER AND LIGHTNING (Rev. 16:18).

The battle will last only *"one day"* (Zech. 14:7), which is the reason it is referred to as *"the Day of the Lord"* or *"that day."* On the very day that Christ returns to Earth and the Battle of Armageddon is fought, the daylight will be neither clear nor dark — much like a partial solar eclipse. But by evening, when the battle is over, it will again be light.

> *"But it shall be one day which shall be known to the LORD, not day, nor night: but it shall come to pass, that at evening time it shall be light"* (Zech. 14:7).

NATURE OF THE BATTLE

By this time the Antichrist will have moved his headquarters from Babylon to Jerusalem. He will desecrate the Temple and break his covenant with the Jews. His desire at this time will be to annihilate Israel, which will be his *"final solution."* He will hate Israel with an irrational, blind, Satan-inspired hatred.

> *"Therefore he shall go forth with great fury to destroy, and utterly to make away many"* (Dan. 11:44).

After the Antichrist has conquered all the countries of the Old Roman

109

Empire (that is, the 10-kingdom confederacy), the armies of Russia —
allied perhaps with China, Japan, and India (the North and the East) — will
trouble him (Dan. 11:41-44). They will see him accomplishing his goal of
world conquest, and they will band together to stop him.

Of course, they will not be able to do this, because as the Antichrist
marches against them, he will *"with great fury"* destroy them and take
over their countries and their armies himself. After he has defeated these
enemies, they will join forces under him and march against Israel for the
Battle of Armageddon (Ezek., Chpts. 38 and 39).

Ezekiel 38:2 refers to the Antichrist as . . .

"Gog . . . the chief prince of Meshech and Tubal."

The evil thought of Gog will be to go up against the Jews who dwell safely
and are at rest in their own Land . . .

"To take a spoil" (Ezek. 38:11-13).

When he comes into Palestine, he will be turned back and completely destroyed by the Second Coming of Christ, even before he can take all of
Jerusalem, the Holy City (Zech. 14:1-5; II Thess. 1:7-10; Jude, Vss. 14-
15; Rev. 19:11-21).

We know, of course, that the Antichrist will be Devil-inspired, Devil-
influenced, and Devil-controlled. According to Revelation 13:2 it is the
Devil who gives him . . .

"his power, and his seat, and great authority."

So, there is no question that he will be an instrument of Satan.

However, we are told further in Revelation 16:13-14 that he will be
aided and abetted in his ambitions by unclean spirits that will inspire the
nations to fight God's chosen People and, ultimately, Christ Himself. Just
as King Ahab in the Old Testament was lured into battle by a lying spirit
(II Chron. 18:18-22), so these political heads will be lured into the Battle of
Armageddon alongside the Antichrist by unclean spirits.

COMBATANTS IN THE BATTLE

The Battle of Armageddon will be unprecedented in many ways. It will
be not only an extensive battle, but a spiritual battle. Lining up together on
one side will be the Devil, the Antichrist, and the armies of Earth. Lining up
together on the other side will be Jesus Christ Himself, the Nation of Israel,

and the Armies of Heaven. (Read Zech., Chpt. 14; Ezek., Chpts. 38-39; II Thess. 1:7-10; Rev. 12:7-12; 16:13-16; 19:11-14; 20:1-3.)

The Antichrist, also called Gog, will come from Syria. We know this from the Prophet Daniel, who saw the *"little horn"* coming out of one of the four divisions of the Grecian Empire (Dan. 8:8-9, 21-23). These four divisions are known today as Greece, Turkey, Syria, and Egypt. If the Antichrist is to come from one of these four, then, of course, he cannot come from the East (the Orient, the isles of the sea), the West (Europe or America), or the South (Africa, Australia).

The Bible refers to him specifically as . . .

"the king of the north" (Dan. 11:40)

. . . meaning Syria. This *"king of the north"* will . . .

1. DO ACCORDING TO HIS OWN WILL (Dan. 11:36; 7:25; 8:24; II Thess. 2:3-4; Rev. 13:5-7);

2. EXALT HIMSELF ABOVE EVERY GOD (Dan. 7:25; 11:36-37; 8:25; II Thess. 2:4; Rev., Chpt. 13);

3. SPEAK MARVELOUS THINGS AGAINST THE GOD OF GODS (Dan. 7:8, 11, 20, 25; 11:36; II Thess. 2:4; Rev. 13:5-6);

4. PROSPER UNTIL THE INDIGNATION BE ACCOM-PLISHED (Dan. 8:9-27; 11:36; II Thess. 2:8; Rev. 19:11-21);

5. REFUSE TO SERVE THE GOD OF HIS FATHERS (Dan. 7:25; 8:25; 11:37; Jn. 5:43; II Thess. 2:4; Rev. 13:1-7);

6. HONOR A GOD WHOM HIS FATHERS KNEW NOT (Dan. 8:24; 11:38-39; II Thess. 2:4; Rev. 13:1-4);

7. LIVE IN THE LAST DAYS AND SUCCESSFULLY CON-QUER KEY LANDS (Dan. 7:8-26; 11:40-42; II Thess. 2:4; Rev. 11:1-2; 12:1-17; 13:1-18);

8. ESTABLISH HIS THRONE IN JERUSALEM (Dan. 9:27; 11:45; II Thess. 2:4; Rev. 11:1-2; 12:1-17; 13:1-18);

9. CAUSE THE GREATEST TIME OF TROUBLE THE EARTH HAS EVER SEEN (Dan. 7:21-27; 8:19-25; 9:27; 12:1; Mat., Chpt. 24; II Thess. 2:8-12; Rev., Chpt. 13; 15:2-4);

10. MAKE WAR ON ISRAEL (Dan. 7:21-26; 8:24; 12:7; Mat., Chpt. 24; Rev., Chpt. 13);

11. SET UP THE ABOMINATION THAT MAKES DESOLATE (Dan. 8:11; 9:27; 11:31; Mat. 24:15; II Thess. 2:4; Rev., Chpt. 13); AND,

12. COME TO HIS END AND NONE CAN HELP HIM (Dan. 7:8-27; 8:25; 11:45; II Thess. 2:8; Rev. 19:11-21; 20:10).

With the Antichrist (also called Gog, the King of the North, the Little Horn, the Beast) will be an army made up of the following:

1. ROSH (Ezek. 39:1, Septuagint);

2. MESHECH (Ezek. 39:1);

3. TUBAL (Ezek. 39:1);

4. PERSIA (Ezek. 38:5);

5. ETHIOPIA (Ezek. 38:5);

6. LIBYA (Ezek. 38:5);

7. GOMER (Ezek. 38:6);

8. TOGARMAH (Ezek. 38:6);

9. MANY PEOPLE (Ezek. 38:6, 9);

10. TEN KINGDOMS (Dan. 7:23-24; Rev. 17:12-17);

11. MANY COUNTRIES (Dan. 11:41-43);

12. COUNTRIES EAST AND NORTH OF THE 10 KINGDOMS (Dan. 11:44);

13. MULTITUDES (Joel 3:11-14);

14. ALL NATIONS (Zech. 14:1-5);

15. KINGS OF THE EARTH (Rev. 16:13-16; 19:19-21); AND,

16. WHOLE WORLD (Rev. 16:13-16).

Against this unlikely horde will come the Armies of Heaven, led by Jesus Christ Himself (Isa. 63:1-5; Zech. 14:1-5; Mat. 24:29-31; II Thess. 1:7-10, Jude, Vss. 14-15; Rev. 11:15; 19:11-21).

Revelation, Chapter 19 gives the breathtaking description of the Lord as He arrives on Planet Earth to defeat the Antichrist forces.

"And I saw Heaven opened, and behold a white horse; and

He Who sat upon him was called Faithful and True, and in Righteousness He does Judge and make war.

"His Eyes were as a flame of fire, and on His Head were many crowns; and He had a Name written, that no man knew, but He Himself.

"And He was clothed with a vesture dipped in Blood: and His Name is called The Word of God.

"And the Armies which were in Heaven followed Him upon white horses, clothed in fine linen, white and clean.

"And out of His Mouth goes a sharp sword, that with it He should smite the nations: and He shall rule them with a rod of iron: and He treads the winepress of the fierceness and wrath of Almighty God.

"And He has on His vesture and on His Thigh a Name written, KING OF KINGS, AND LORD OF LORDS.

"And I saw an Angel standing in the sun; and he cried with a loud voice, saying to all the fowls who fly in the midst of Heaven, Come and gather yourselves together unto the supper of the Great God;

"That you may eat the flesh of kings, and the flesh of captains, and the flesh of mighty men, and the flesh of horses, and of them who sit on them, and the flesh of all men, both free and bond, both small and great" (Rev. 19:11-18).

The Prophet Isaiah described:

"Who is this Who comes from Edom, with dyed garments from Bozrah? He Who is glorious in His apparel, travelling in the greatness of His Strength? I Who speak in Righteousness, mighty to save.

"Wherefore are You red in Your apparel, and Your garments like him who treads in the winefat?

"I have trodden the winepress alone; and of the people there was none with Me: for I will tread them in My Anger, and trample them in My Fury; and their blood shall be sprinkled upon My garments, and I will stain all My raiment.

"For the day of vengeance is in My Heart, and the year of My Redeemed is come.

"And I looked, and there was none to help; and I wondered that there was none to uphold: therefore My Own Arm brought Salvation unto Me; and My Fury, it upheld Me.

"And I will tread down the people in My Anger, and make

them drunk in My Fury, and I will bring down their strength to the Earth" (Isa. 63:1-6).

A VERITABLE BLOODBATH

"Gog," "the man of sin," "the son of perdition," "the beast," "the little horn" all speak of a man who will come in the Last Days and who will make an almost successful bid for world domination, while simultaneously trying to annihilate Israel. With his millions of recruits from Russia, China, Asia, and Europe, he will come down to cover the Nation of Israel like a cloud.

Every major television network in the world, no doubt, will be there to record this climactic moment of history. Through the miracle of satellite, pictures of the Antichrist's mighty armies could reach the homes of millions of people and all nations throughout the world. This great event could unfold before the eyes of the whole world!

To the Prophet Zechariah the Lord revealed:

"For I will gather all nations against Jerusalem to battle" (Zech. 14:2).

The world will watch raptly as Israel tries to defend herself. This tiny country of a few million Jews has stood against hundreds of thousands of Arabs and Miracle after Miracle has occurred. But this will be the ultimate battle, a battle of such horror it beggars description.

The Antichrist will fling his armies against all Israel, but especially against Jerusalem. It will be door-to-door fighting, house-to-house confrontation, and the city will be leveled. The Jews will have their back to the wall. *"Half of the city"* (Zech. 14:2) will fall. At that moment — no doubt, under the eye of the TV camera — the Jews will realize that the die is cast. There is no Hope. All resistance is pointless. They will lose.

A pall of smoke will hang over the Holy City. Flames will leap from house to house, building to building, embassy to embassy. Artillery will roar. Jets will scream. The City of Peace will be turned into a city of blood.

The Antichrist will spur his armies to push even harder. They will sense victory — that nothing can stop them! From their point of view the hated Jew will be annihilated once and for all. Hope of the True Messiah, Jesus Christ, will be eliminated from the Earth. . . .

Before he died, David Ben-Gurion, Israeli statesman and first Prime Minister, was asked, *"What is Israel's future? What is Israel's hope?"*

The white-haired old sage looked down toward the ground and finally answered, with a faraway look in his eyes, *"The hope of Israel is the coming of the Messiah."*

In that moment, when Israel little dreams, they will begin to cry. They will weep as never before for Messiah to come. Their sudden cry will fill the Holy City in the midst of the din, as screams of cannon shells, mortar bursts, and machine gunfire fill the air. They will wail like babies screaming in pain. They will beg. They will plead. They will cry for Messiah to come.

> *"And it shall come to pass at the same time when Gog shall come against the land of Israel, saith the Lord GOD, that My Fury shall come up in My Face.*
>
> *"For in My jealousy and in the fire of My wrath have I spoken, Surely in that day there shall be a great shaking in the land of Israel;*
>
> *"So that the fishes of the sea, and the fowls of the Heaven, and the beasts of the field, and all creeping things that creep upon the Earth, and all the men who are upon the face of the Earth, shall shake at My Presence, and the mountains shall be thrown down, and the steep places shall fall, and every wall shall fall to the ground.*
>
> *"And I will call for a sword against him throughout all My mountains, saith the Lord GOD: every man's sword shall be against his brother.*
>
> *"And I will plead against him with pestilence and with blood; and I will rain upon him, and upon his bands, and upon the many people who are with him, an overflowing rain, and great hailstones, fire, and brimstones.*
>
> *"Thus will I magnify Myself, and sanctify Myself; and I will be known in the eyes of many nations, and they shall know that I am the LORD"* (Ezek. 38:18-23).

The Prophet Zechariah affirmed:

> *"Then shall the LORD go forth, and fight against those nations, as when He fought in the day of battle.*
>
> *"And this shall be the plague wherewith the LORD will smite all the people who have fought against Jerusalem; Their flesh shall consume away while they stand upon their feet, and their eyes shall consume away in their holes, and their tongue shall consume away in their mouth.*
>
> *"And it shall come to pass in that day, that a great tumult from the LORD shall be among them; and they shall lay hold*

*everyone on the hand of his neighbour, and his hand shall rise
up against the hand of his neighbour. . . .*

*"And so shall be the plague of the horse, of the mule, of
the camel, and of the ass, and of all the beasts that shall be in
these tents, as this plague"* (Zech. 14:3, 12-15).

Everything and everybody, including fish life, animal life, human life,
plant life, will be affected. This is referred to in the Book of Revelation as
the harvest of the Earth. And it will be a veritable bloodbath.

*"And another Angel came out of the Temple, crying with a
loud voice to Him Who sat on the cloud, Thrust in your sickle,
and reap: for the time is come for you to reap; for the harvest
of the Earth is ripe.*

*"And the Angel thrust in his sickle into the Earth, and gath-
ered the vine of the Earth, and cast it into the great winepress
of the Wrath of God.*

*"And the winepress was trodden without the city, and
BLOOD CAME OUT OF THE WINEPRESS, EVEN UNTO
THE HORSE BRIDLES, BY THE SPACE OF A THOUSAND
AND SIX HUNDRED FURLONGS"* (Rev. 14:15, 19-20).

As the television cameras record this appalling series of events, no
doubt the TV announcer will be struck tongue-tied as he tries to comprehend what is occurring. No one will understand.

Let us imagine the cameras suddenly panning upward — millions of TV
sets around the world tuned in, waiting breathlessly for the live, on-the-
scene reports — as the sky is filled, rank upon rank, troop upon troop,
regiment upon regiment, with the Heavenly Host of the Lord Jesus Christ
returning in the clouds.

Every Saint who has ever lived will be there, riding upon white horses
as they come back to Earth to fight this momentous battle. When this
happens, the sky will radiate an eerie, diffused light. The battle, which lasts
one day, will be somewhat like Joshua's battle of old (Josh. 10:13). At
evening time it will be light (Zech. 14:7).

The Lord will use this extended light — half-light — to rain pestilence
with blood upon the Antichrist's forces. He will rain upon him and upon
his bands an overflowing rain, and great hailstones, fire, and brimstone.
In this terrible conflict the blood will run to the horses' bridle for 175 miles
(Rev. 14:20). Many men will die. And Israel — against all odds, just as in
days of yesteryear — will be victorious, because the Lord Himself will
defend her and whip the enemy and get her the Victory!

RESULTS OF THE BATTLE

Ezekiel, Chapter 39 describes for us the awesome results of this battle.

"Behold, I am against you, O Gog, the chief prince of Meshech and Tubal:

"And I will turn you back, and leave but the sixth part of you, and will cause you to come up from the north parts, and will bring you upon the mountains of Israel:

"And I will smite your bow out of your left hand, and will cause your arrows to fall out of your right hand.

"You shall fall upon the mountains of Israel, you, and all your bands, and the people that is with you: I will give you unto the ravenous birds of every sort, and to the beasts of the field to be devoured.

"You shall fall upon the open field: for I have spoken it, saith the Lord GOD.

"And I will send a fire on Magog, and among them who dwell carelessly in the isles: and they shall know that I am the LORD.

"So will I make My Holy Name known in the midst of My People Israel; and I will not let them pollute My Holy Name any more: and the heathen shall know that I am the LORD, the Holy One in Israel" (Ezek. 39:1-7).

Millions of people will die. *Millions!* Out of *every million* persons in the Antichrist's army *833,333* will die. Only a sixth part of men under the Antichrist will be spared. This means that out of *every million* persons in the enemy forces *166,667* will live. No battle in the history of the world has witnessed such devastation!

After the Battle of Armageddon it will take *seven months* to bury the dead. Before most of the decomposed bodies can be disposed of, the stench will fill the land.

"And it shall come to pass in that day, that I will give unto Gog a place there of graves in Israel, the valley of the passengers on the east of the sea: and IT SHALL STOP THE NOSES OF THE PASSENGERS: and there shall they bury Gog and all his multitude: and they shall call it THE VALLEY OF HAMON-GOG.

"AND SEVEN MONTHS SHALL THE HOUSE OF ISRAEL BE BURYING OF THEM, that they may cleanse the land.

"Yea, all the people of the land shall bury them; and it shall be to them a renown the day that I shall be glorified, saith the Lord GOD.

"AND THEY SHALL SEVER OUT MEN OF CONTINUAL EMPLOYMENT, PASSING THROUGH THE LAND TO BURY WITH THE PASSENGERS THOSE WHO REMAIN UPON THE FACE OF THE EARTH, to cleanse it: after the end of seven months shall they search.

"And the passengers who pass through the land, when any sees a man's bone, then shall he set up a sign by it, till the buriers have buried it in the valley of Hamon-gog" (Ezek. 39:11-15).

Also, after the Battle of Armageddon it will take years to dispose of the weapons forfeited by the dead. The people of Israel will be picking up discarded weapons and using them for firewood for *seven years*:

"And they who dwell in the cities of Israel shall go forth, and shall set on fire and burn the weapons, both the shields and the bucklers, the bows and the arrows, and the handstaves, and the spears, and THEY SHALL BURN THEM WITH FIRE SEVEN YEARS:

"So that they shall take no wood out of the field, neither cut down any out of the forests; for they shall burn the weapons with fire: and they shall spoil those who spoiled them, and rob those who robbed them, saith the Lord GOD" (Ezek. 39:9-10).

Just as the people of Israel *"spoiled"* their enemy Egypt in the days of Moses (Ex. 12:35-36), so they will *"spoil"* their enemy in the days of the returning Christ. We do not know exactly the type of equipment and fuel that will be provided at this time, but from the description we can surmise that the battle will be a land war, not a nuclear war (as some persons may teach). The weapons will be used as fuel in lieu of wood from the forests. In modern cities, no doubt, people will use natural gas and electricity, but in the outlying areas, the rural and suburban regions, there will still be people depending on wood and other materials for their energy needs.

Also, after the Battle of Armageddon it will take *seven months* for the birds and beasts of prey to help in cleansing the land:

"Speak unto every feathered fowl, and to every beast of the field, Assemble yourselves, and come; gather yourselves on every side to My Sacrifice that I do sacrifice for you, even a great sacrifice upon the mountains of Israel, that you may eat

flesh, and drink blood.

"Thus you shall be filled at My table with horses and chariots, with mighty men, and with all men of war, saith the Lord GOD" (Ezek. 39:17, 20).

John the Revelator described:

"And I saw an Angel standing in the sun; and he cried with a loud voice, saying to all the fowls who fly in the midst of Heaven, Come and gather yourselves together unto the supper of the Great God;

"That you may eat the flesh of kings, and the flesh of captains, and the flesh of mighty men, and the flesh of horses, and of them who sit on them, and the flesh of all men, both free and bond, both small and great.

"And I saw the beast, and the kings of the Earth, and THEIR ARMIES, GATHERED TOGETHER TO MAKE WAR AGAINST HIM WHO SAT ON THE HORSE, AND AGAINST HIS ARMY.

"And the beast was taken, and with him the false prophet. . . .

"And the remnant were slain with the sword of Him Who sat upon the horse, which sword proceeded out of His Mouth: AND ALL THE FOWLS WERE FILLED WITH THEIR FLESH" (Rev. 19:17-21).

"For wheresoever the carcase is, there will the eagles be gathered together" (Mat. 24:28).

The Battle of Armageddon will mean the total defeat of satanic forces under the Antichrist. The Beast and the False Prophet will be condemned to the Lake of Fire forever (Rev. 19:20). Satan and his henchmen will be sentenced to the abyss for 1,000 years (Rev. 20:1-7). On the other hand, Israel will be delivered and vindicated and the Millennial Kingdom will begin (Rev., Chpts. 19 and 20).

PURPOSE OF THE BATTLE

The purpose of Satan and the Antichrist in this battle will be simple: (1) To take a prey, meaning Israel (Ezek. 38:8-13), (2) To stop Christ from taking possession of the Earth, and (3) To avert their own doom.

The Purpose of God, however, will be manifold:

1. TO DELIVER ISRAEL (Ezek. 39:25-29);

2. TO BRING AN END TO THE TIME OF THE GENTILES (Rev. 11:1-2; Lk. 21:24);

3. TO PUNISH THE NATIONS FOR THEIR PERSECUTION OF ISRAEL (Mat. 25:31-46);

4. TO SET UP THE MILLENNIAL KINGDOM (Dan. 2:44-45; Rev. 11:15);

5. TO RID THE EARTH OF ALL REBELLION (Rev. 20:7-10);

6. TO MAGNIFY HIMSELF IN THE EYES OF MANY NATIONS (Ezek. 38:23; 39:7);

7. TO REVEAL HIMSELF TO ISRAEL (Ezek. 39:22);

8. TO REVEAL HIMSELF TO THE HEATHEN (Ezek. 39:21, 23);

9. TO GATHER TOGETHER ALL THINGS IN CHRIST (Eph. 1:10); AND,

10. TO GIVE MAN ONE FINAL CHANCE TO REPENT BEFORE THE JUDGMENT (Rev., Chpt. 20; II Pet. 3:10-13).

In the final analysis the Battle of Armageddon will usher in the great Kingdom called the Millennial Reign, when Jesus Christ will set up that Kingdom . . .

"which shall never be destroyed" (Dan. 2:44).

Then . . .

"the desert shall rejoice, and blossom as the rose" (Isa. 35:1) . . . and . . .

"the Earth shall be full of the Knowledge of the LORD, as the waters cover the sea" (Isa. 11:9).

As John the Revelator said:

"Even so, come, Lord Jesus" (Rev. 22:20).

Chapter 4

The Second Coming Of Christ

CHAPTER FOUR

THE SECOND COMING OF CHRIST

The Second Coming of Jesus Christ is one of the most attested truths of Scripture. Just prior to the Ascension, Jesus was asked by the Disciples:

>*"Lord, will You at this time restore again the Kingdom to Israel?"* (Acts 1:6).

The Disciples, like all Jews of their day, expected that when the Messiah came, He would establish the long-awaited Messianic Kingdom on Earth. They believed that all the Old Testament Prophecies foretold that when the Messiah came, Israel would be restored to her former glory. To the Disciples it appeared that the purpose of the Resurrection was to establish the Kingdom they had been discussing for 40 days (Acts 1:3).
Jesus' answer was . . .

>*"It is not for you to know the times or the seasons, which the Father has put in His Own Power"* (Acts 1:7).

Just as Jesus finished uttering these words, He immediately disappeared from the Disciples (Acts 1:10). How surprised they must have been! To assay their fears . . .

>*"two men stood by them in white apparel;*
>*"Which also said, You men of Galilee, why do you stand gazing up into Heaven? THIS SAME JESUS, which is taken up from you into Heaven, SHALL SO COME IN LIKE MANNER as you have seen Him go into Heaven"* (Acts 1:10-11).

Just as General Douglas MacArthur kept his promise that *"I shall return,"* following the Japanese invasion of the Philippines, even more surely Jesus will return as the Angel announced to the onlooking Disciples.
Not only will He return, but He will come *"in like manner"* (cf. Zech. 14:1-4, 9; Jn. 14:1-3). Even as He ascended . . .

>*"and a cloud received Him out of their sight"* (Acts 1:9)

. . . so . . .

"He comes with clouds; and every eye shall see Him" (Rev 1:7).

MANNER OF HIS COMING

Many phrases, words, and expressions are used in Scripture to describe the manner of His Coming.

1. HIS COMING WILL BE SPEEDY.

   "For as the lightning comes out of the east, and shines even unto the west; so shall also the coming of the Son of Man be" (Mat. 24:27).

2. HIS COMING WILL BE WITH POWER AND GREAT GLORY.

   "And then shall appear the sign of the Son of Man in Heaven: and then shall all the tribes of the Earth mourn, and they shall see the Son of Man coming in the clouds of Heaven with Power and great glory" (Mat. 24:30).

3. HIS COMING WILL BE WITH BRIGHTNESS AND FIRE.

   "The Lord Jesus shall be revealed from Heaven with His mighty Angels,
   "In flaming fire taking vengeance on them who know not God . . .
   "When He shall come" (II Thess. 1:7-8, 10).

4. HIS COMING WILL BE WITH VENGEANCE AND GREAT WRATH.

   "And it shall come to pass in that day, saith the LORD, that. . . .
   "I will execute vengeance in anger and fury upon the heathen, such as they have not heard" (Mic. 5:10, 15).

5. HIS COMING WILL BE AS JUDGE AND KING.

   "When the Son of Man shall come in His Glory, and all the Holy Angels with Him, then shall He sit upon the Throne of His Glory" (Mat. 25:31; cf. 25:31-46).

6. HIS COMING WILL BE WITH SAINTS AND ANGELS.

"And the LORD my God shall come, and all the Saints with you" (Zech. 14:5).

"And He shall send His Angels with a great sound of a trumpet, and they shall gather together His Elect from the four winds, from one end of Heaven to the other" (Mat. 24:31).

7. HIS COMING WILL BE SUDDEN.

"For yourselves know perfectly that the Day of the Lord so comes as a thief in the night.
"For when they shall say, Peace and safety; then sudden destruction comes upon them . . . and they shall not escape" (I Thess. 5:2-3).

8. HIS COMING WILL BE LITERAL.

"And His Feet shall stand in that day upon the Mount of Olives, which is before Jerusalem on the east, and the Mount of Olives shall cleave in the midst thereof toward the east and toward the west, and there shall be a very great valley; and half of the mountain shall remove toward the north, and half of it toward the south" (Zech. 14:4).

9. HIS COMING WILL BE VISIBLE.

"Behold, He comes with clouds; and every eye shall see Him, and they also which pierced Him: and all kindreds of the Earth shall wail because of Him" (Rev. 1:7).

10. HIS COMING WILL BE WITH CLOUDS.

"Jesus said unto him, You have said: nevertheless I say unto you, Hereafter shall you see the Son of Man sitting on the Right Hand of Power, and coming in the clouds of Heaven" (Mat. 26:64).

Of course, other Scriptures may be cross-referenced such as Ezekiel, Chapters 38 and 39; Daniel 7:13-14; Malachi 4:1-6; Jude, Vss. 14-15; Revelation 14:14-20; 17:14; 19:11-21.

DESCRIPTION OF CHRIST AT HIS COMING

The Bible gives several contrasts between Christ's First and Second Advents.

In His First Advent He came *"meek"* and *"lowly"* (Zech. 9:9; Mat. 21:5), riding a colt.

In His Second Advent He will come *"with power and great glory"* (Mat. 24:30), riding a white horse (Rev. 19:11).

In His First Advent . . .

"there is no beauty that we should desire Him" (Isa. 53:2).

In His Second Advent it will be said:

"how great is His beauty!" (Zech. 9:17).

In His First Advent He was . . .

"despised and rejected of men; a Man of sorrows, and acquainted with grief . . . and we esteemed Him not" (Isa. 53:3).

In His Second Advent He will be lauded and worshipped. Every knee will bow and every tongue will confess that He is Lord to the Glory of God the Father (Phil. 2:9-11; Rev. 5:13).

In His First Advent He was stricken, smitten of God, and afflicted (Isa. 53:4).

In His Second Advent He will be called:

"Wonderful, Counsellor, The Mighty God, The Everlasting Father, The Prince of Peace.

"Of the increase of His Government and Peace there shall be no end" (Isa. 9:6-7).

In His First Advent He was subject to human authority (Lk. 2:51). In His Second Advent He will be subject to no one:

"And He has on His vesture and on His Thigh a Name written, KING OF KINGS, AND LORD OF LORDS" (Rev. 19:16).

In His First Advent He was subject to the frailties of human flesh and the wiles of the enemy (Mat. 4:1-11; Heb. 2:18; 4:15).

In His Second Advent He will exercise full dominion over man and evil (Dan. 7:13-14; Zech. 9:10; Rev. 19:15).

In His First Advent He was poor (Zech. 9:9; II Cor. 8:9).

In His Second Advent He will be rich (Rev., Chpts. 21-22; II Cor. 8:9).

In His First Advent He allowed Himself to be beaten, smitten, crucified, and to die (Mat., Chpt. 27; Isa., Chpt. 53).

In His Second Advent He will reveal His Triumph (Col. 2:15) by heading up the Armies of Heaven against the enemy (Rev. 19:11-21).

In His First Advent He was, as was supposed, the lowly carpenter, son of Joseph (Lk. 4:22).

In His Second Advent He will proclaim to the world His True Identity:

"KING OF KINGS, LORD OF LORDS" (Rev. 19:16).

In His First Advent He preached good tidings, ministered to the brokenhearted, comforted the oppressed (Isa. 61:1; Lk. 4:18).

In His Second Advent He will tread down the people in His Anger, and *"make them drunk"* in His Fury, and bring down their strength to the Earth (Isa. 63:1-6; Rev. 19:15).

Daniel, Chapter 10, Revelation, Chapter 1, and Revelation, Chapter 19 give us insight into the appearance of the preincarnate and postincarnate Christ.

The Prophet Daniel saw . . .

"a certain man clothed in linen, Whose Loins were girded with fine gold of Uphaz:

"His Body also was like the beryl, and His Face as the appearance of lightning, and His Eyes as lamps of fire, and His Arms and His Feet like in colour to polished brass, and the Voice of His Words like the voice of a multitude" (Dan. 10:5-7).

The Apostle John saw . . .

"One like unto the Son of Man, clothed with a garment down to the Foot, and girt about the Paps with a Golden Girdle.

"His Head and His Hairs were white like wool, as white as snow; and His Eyes were as a flame of fire;

"And His Feet like unto fine brass, as if they burned in a furnace; and His Voice as the sound of many waters.

"And He had in His Right Hand Seven Stars: and out of His Mouth went a sharp twoedged Sword: and His Countenance

was as the sun shines in His Strength" (Rev. 1:13-16).

"And I saw Heaven opened, and behold a white horse; and He Who sat upon him was called Faithful and True, and in Righteousness He does judge and make war.

"His Eyes were as a flame of fire, and on His Head were many crowns; and He had a Name written, that no man knew, but He Himself.

"And He was clothed with a vesture dipped in Blood: and His Name is called The Word of God.

"And the armies which were in Heaven followed Him upon white horses, clothed in fine linen, white and clean.

"And out of His Mouth goes a sharp sword, that with it He should smite the nations: and He shall rule them with a rod of iron: and He treads the winepress of the fierceness and Wrath of Almighty God.

"And He has on His vesture and on His Thigh a Name written, KING OF KINGS, AND LORD OF LORDS" (Rev. 19:11-16).

From these Scriptures we learn that at His Coming Christ will be clothed *"in linen,"* clothed *"with a garment down to the foot,"* clothed *"with a vesture dipped in blood,"* clothed *"in fine linen, white and clean."* His Belt will be *"fine gold."* His Arms and Feet will be the color of *"fine brass."* His Countenance will be like the sun; His Eyes, *"lamps of fire"*; His Voice, *"like the voice of a multitude"* or *"as the sound of many waters"*; His Mouth, *"a sharp sword."* Everything about Him will reveal power and awesome, absolute authority!

A LITERAL COMING

The Second Coming of Christ will coincide with other events on the prophetic agenda. It will be a day of horrible destruction, in which the Battle of Armageddon will be fought. It will also be a day of National Repentance, as Israel learns that the Son of Man, Jesus Christ of Nazareth, is truly her long-awaited Messiah. It will also be a day of Judgment upon the Earth and catastrophic changes in the Earth's surface.

Just prior to Christ's Return, Jerusalem will be taken by the Antichrist, the houses will be rifled, the women will be ravished, and the city will go into captivity (Zech. 14:1-2; Mat., Chpt. 24). Suddenly Christ will appear from Heaven, with His Armies, and defeat the Antichrist's forces in a one-day battle. At this time He will take over the kingdoms of this world and set up His Own Kingdom, to reign eternally.

The Feet of Jesus Christ — with the nail prints in them — will literally touch down on the Mount of Olives, near Jerusalem. The mountain will split into east and west, creating a great valley (Zech. 14:4). Israel will flee as she fled before the earthquake in the days of Uzziah, king of Judah.

The landscape will be so altered that a new river will emerge out of Jerusalem. Half of it will flow toward the *"former sea"* (the Dead Sea) and half of it will flow toward the *"hinder sea"* (the Mediterranean Sea), all year long, *"in summer and in winter"* (Zech. 14:8). Much of the great desert south of Jerusalem will become a great plain (Isa., Chpt. 35) and will be inhabited. Jerusalem itself will be raised (Zech. 14:10).

The realization that this same Jesus has defeated the Antichrist's forces and brought about Salvation for the Jews will be eye-opening! In that day when Jesus comes with His Armies to take over the kingdoms of this world, Israel will turn to Him with a whole heart, with fasting, with weeping, with mourning, with national repentance. No doubt, the Jews will wail with bitterness because of the long millennia when they *looked* for a coming Messiah and did not realize that they were *overlooking* the very Christ.

"And it shall come to pass in that day, that I will seek to destroy all the nations that come against Jerusalem.

"And I will pour upon the house of David and upon the inhabitants of Jerusalem, the Spirit of Grace and of Supplications: and they shall look upon Me Whom they have pierced, and they shall mourn for Him, as one mourns for his only son, and shall be in bitterness for Him, as one that is in bitterness for his firstborn" (Zech. 12:9-10).

This will be the day of Israel's national conversion, at the Second Coming of Christ. It will also be the fulfillment of Joel's Prophecy (Joel 2:28) and the time that a Nation will be born in a day (Isa. 66:7-8). All Israel will be Saved at this time, when the Redeemer comes from the Heavenly Mount Zion to the earthly Mount Zion.

"In that day there shall be a fountain opened to the house of David and to the inhabitants of Jerusalem for sin and for uncleanness" (Zech. 13:1).

This Fountain is that same Fountain that is opened for the Christian today (Mat. 26:28; Col. 1:20; 2:14-17; I Pet. 1:5; 5:8-10). The Jews will finally accept the Cross of Jesus Christ as the only Way of Salvation and deliverance from sin and uncleanness and the only Way of national preservation. This Fountain filled with Blood, drawn from Immanuel's Veins, will cleanse away all sin and stain!

A DAY OF JUDGMENT

Not everyone living at that time will even know that Christ has returned to Earth, until, like we today, they hear it on the airwaves or on the streets.

This will be a time not when Christ deals with individuals, but when He deals with nations. At this time Christ will call the nations before Him to give an account. This will not be the Great White Throne Judgment, when everyone, small and great, answers to God for the things done in this life. The Great White Throne Judgment will take place after the Millennium. This Judgment of the Nations will be a national Judgment that takes place when Christ returns to set up His Kingdom.

To contrast:

1. THE JUDGMENT OF THE NATIONS WILL INVOLVE THOSE NATIONS LIVING WHEN CHRIST RETURNS.

"When the Son of Man shall come in His Glory, and all the Holy Angels with Him, then shall He sit upon the Throne of His Glory:
"And before Him shall be gathered all nations . . ." (Mat. 25:31-32; Jude, Vss. 14-15; Rev. 19:11).

THE GREAT WHITE THRONE JUDGMENT WILL INVOLVE ALL THE WICKED FROM TIME IMMEMORIAL.

"And I saw the dead, small and great, stand before God; and the Books were opened: and another Book was opened, which is the Book of Life: and the dead were Judged out of those things which were written in the Books, according to their works.
"And the sea gave up the dead which were in it; and Death and Hell delivered up the dead which were in them: and they were judged every man according to their works" (Rev. 20:12-13; II Pet. 2:4-9).

2. THE JUDGMENT OF THE NATIONS WILL TAKE PLACE BEFORE THE MILLENNIUM.

"When the Son of Man shall come in His Glory . . . then shall He sit upon the Throne of His Glory" (Mat. 25:31; Isa. 66:15-18).

THE GREAT WHITE THRONE JUDGMENT WILL TAKE

PLACE AFTER THE MILLENNIUM.

"And when the thousand years are expired . . . I saw a Great White Throne . . . and the Books were opened" (Rev. 20:7-12).

3. AT THE JUDGMENT OF THE NATIONS CHRIST WILL SIT IN JUDGMENT.

"For the Father judges no man, but has committed all judgment unto the Son" (Jn. 5:22; Acts 17:31; Mat. 25:31-32; II Tim. 4:1).

AT THE GREAT WHITE THRONE JUDGMENT GOD WILL SIT IN JUDGMENT.

"And I saw the dead, small and great, stand before God" (Rev. 20:12; Heb. 12:23; 13:4).

4. THE JUDGMENT OF THE NATIONS WILL TAKE PLACE ON EARTH.

"Then shall all the trees of the wood rejoice. Before the LORD: for He comes, for He comes to judge the Earth" (Ps. 96:12-13; Mat. 25:31-32).

THE GREAT WHITE THRONE JUDGMENT WILL TAKE PLACE IN HEAVEN.

"Behold, a Throne was set in Heaven, and One sat on the Throne. And I saw a Great White Throne, and Him Who sat on it . . . and the Books were opened" (Rev. 4:2; 20:11-12).

5. AT THE JUDGMENT OF THE NATIONS SOME WILL BE SAVED, SOME WILL BE DAMNED.

"Then shall the King say unto them on His Right Hand, Come, you blessed of My Father, inherit the Kingdom prepared for you from the foundation of the world:
"Then shall He say also unto them on the Left Hand, Depart from Me, you cursed, into everlasting fire" (Mat. 25:34, 41).

AT THE GREAT WHITE THRONE JUDGMENT ALL WILL

BE DAMNED.

"Blessed and Holy is he who has part in the First Resurrection: on such the second death has no power. . . .

"And I saw the dead, small and great, stand before God . . . and the dead were judged . . . every man according to their works.

"And Death and Hell were cast into the Lake of Fire. This is the second death.

"And whosoever was not found written in the Book of Life was cast into the Lake of Fire" (Rev. 20:6-15).

6. NO RESURRECTION WILL PRECEDE THE JUDGMENT OF THE NATIONS.

"And it shall come to pass in the last days, that the mountain of the LORD's house shall be established in the top of the mountains . . . and all nations shall flow unto it. . . . And He shall judge among the nations" (Isa. 2:2-4; Mat. 25:31-46).

BEFORE THE GREAT WHITE THRONE JUDGMENT THERE WILL BE A RESURRECTION OF THE UNRIGHTEOUS DEAD.

"And the sea gave up the dead which were in it; and Death and Hell delivered up the dead which were in them: and they were Judged every man according to their works" (Rev. 20:13).

7. AT THE JUDGMENT OF THE NATIONS NO BOOK WILL BE OPENED.

"Let the heathen be wakened, and come up to the valley of Jehoshaphat: for there will I sit to judge all the heathen round about" (Joel 3:12; Mat. 25:31-46).

AT THE GREAT WHITE THRONE JUDGMENT THE BOOKS WILL BE OPENED AND THE DEAD WILL BE JUDGED OUT OF THOSE BOOKS.

"I beheld till the thrones were cast down, and the Ancient of days did sit. . . .

"A fiery stream issued and came forth from before Him: thousand thousands ministered unto Him, and ten thousand

times ten thousand stood before Him: the judgment was set, and the Books were opened" (Dan. 7:9-10; Rev. 20:12).

8. THE JUDGMENT OF THE NATIONS WILL CONCERN BASICALLY THE ATTITUDE OF THE NATIONS TOWARD ISRAEL.

"Now the Lord had said unto Abram . . .
"I will make of you a great Nation, and I will bless you . . .
"And I will bless them who bless you, and curse him who curses you" (Gen. 12:1-3; Isa. 66:18-21; Mat. 10:5-15).

THE GREAT WHITE THRONE JUDGMENT WILL CONCERN ALL KINDS OF SINS OF ALL KINDS OF MEN.

"For God shall bring every work into judgment, with every secret thing, whether it be good, or whether it be evil" (Eccl. 12:14; Ps. 7:11-16; 9:15-17; I Pet. 1:17; Rom. 1:32; Rev. 20:12).

9. THE JUDGMENT OF THE NATIONS WILL SEPARATE THE GOOD FROM THE BAD, THE SHEEP FROM THE GOATS.

"And before Him shall be gathered all nations: and He shall separate them one from another, as a shepherd divides his sheep from the goats.
"And He shall set the sheep on His Right Hand, but the goats on the left" (Mat. 25:32-33).

THE GREAT WHITE THRONE JUDGMENT WILL JUDGE ONLY THE BAD.

"For we know Him Who has said, Vengeance belongs unto Me, I will recompense, says the Lord. And again, The Lord shall judge His People.
"It is a fearful thing to fall into the hands of the Living God" (Heb. 10:30-31; Deut. 32:35-36; I Cor. 5:13; Jude, Vs. 6; Rev. 20:13-14).

10. THE JUDGMENT OF THE NATIONS WILL JUDGE GENTILES.

"Behold My Servant, Whom I uphold; My Elect, in Whom

My Soul delights; I have put My Spirit upon Him: He shall bring forth Judgment to the Gentiles" (Isa. 42:1; 2:3-4; Chpt., 4; 66:18-21; Joel 3:12; Mat. 11:20-24).

THE GREAT WHITE THRONE JUDGMENT WILL JUDGE JEW AND GENTILE.

"And I saw another Angel fly in the midst of Heaven, having the everlasting Gospel to preach unto them who dwell on the Earth, and to every nation, and kindred, and tongue, and people,
"Saying with a loud voice, Fear God, and give Glory to Him; for the hour of His Judgment is come" (Rev. 14:6-7; 20:12).

11.   THE JUDGMENT OF THE NATIONS WILL BE NATIONAL.

"And He shall judge among many people, and rebuke strong nations afar off" (Mic. 4:3; Isa. 2:3-4; Mat. 25:31-46).

THE GREAT WHITE THRONE JUDGMENT WILL BE IN-DIVIDUAL.

"And I saw the dead, small and great, stand before God; and the Books were opened" (Rev. 20:12; I Pet. 4:5-6; Eccl. 12:14).

12.   FROM THE JUDGMENT OF THE NATIONS SOME WILL ENTER INTO ETERNAL LIFE.

"Then shall the King say unto them on His Right Hand, Come, you blessed of My Father, inherit the Kingdom prepared for you from the foundation of the world" (Mat. 25:34).

FROM THE GREAT WHITE THRONE JUDGMENT NO ONE WILL ENTER INTO ETERNAL LIFE.

"For he shall have Judgment without Mercy, who has shown no Mercy" (James 2:13; Lk. 12:5; Heb. 10:26-31; Rev. 20:5).

DAWN OF PEACE

The Second Coming of Christ, although a day of destruction and national Judgment, will also be the beginning of a New Age. This New Age will be an era of peace and prosperity for Israel and the world.

In His coming Christ will . . .

1. COME TO ZION (Isa. 59:20; Zech. 14:4);

2. COME TO THEM WHO TURN FROM SIN (Isa. 59:20; Zech. 12:10; 14:1-5; Rom. 11:25-29);

3. MAKE A NEW COVENANT WITH ISRAEL (Isa. 42:6; 49:8; 55:3; 57:8; 59:21; 61:8; Jer. 31:31; Heb. 10:16);

4. POUR OUT HIS SPIRIT (Isa. 32:15; 34:16; 44:3; 59:21; Joel 2:28-32; Zech. 12:10); AND,

5. PUT THE WORDS OF GOD IN THEIR MOUTH (Isa. 59:21).

As a result Israel will . . .

1. SEE WITH THEIR HEART (Isa. 60:5);

2. FLOW TOGETHER AS ONE NATION IN THEIR OWN LAND (Isa. 60:5; Ezek. 37:16-24);

3. FEAR GOD (Isa. 60:5); AND,

4. BE ENLARGED AND BLESSED WITH ABUNDANCE (Isa. 60:5).

DIVINE PURPOSE

God always has a Plan and a Purpose for every Divine activity. With Him nothing happens by chance. All things eventually flow into His Will and Purpose *"unto the praise of His Glory."*

"According to His good pleasure which He has purposed in Himself:
"That in the dispensation of the fulness of times He might gather together in one all things in Christ, both which are in Heaven, and which are on Earth; even in Him:
". . . unto the praise of His Glory" (Eph. 1:9-14).

The Purpose of God in the Second Coming of Christ will be . . .

1. TO TAKE VENGEANCE ON THE UNGODLY (II Thess. 1:7-10; Jude, Vss. 14-15; Rev. 19:11-21);

2. TO JUDGE THE NATIONS (Mat. 25:31-46; Ps. 67:4; 96:10-13; 98:9);

3. TO DELIVER NATIONAL ISRAEL (Zech. 14:4-6; Rom. 11:25-29; Isa. 63:1-6; Mat. 25:31-46; Rev. 19:11-21);

4. TO SET UP HIS KINGDOM (Isa. 9:6-7; Ps. 72; Lk. 1:31-33);

5. TO DELIVER THE CREATION FROM BONDAGE (Isa. 11:1-2; 35:1-8; 65:20-25; Rom. 8:21-24);

6. TO BRING AN END TO LAWLESSNESS (I Cor. 15:24-28; Rev. 2:27; 11:15; 19:11-21);

7. TO ESTABLISH JUSTICE (Ps. 72:11; Isa. 2:1-4; Rev. 20:1-11);

8. TO REBUILD THE TEMPLE (Ezek. 43:7; Zech. 6:12-13);

9. TO MAKE KNOWN THE GLORY OF GOD (Isa. 4:2-6; 35:2; 40:5; 60:1-9; Ezek. 39:21; Mat. 16:27; 25:31);

10. TO BRING UNIVERSAL PEACE AND PROSPERITY (Isa. 2:1-4; 35:1-8; Mic. 4:1-7);

11. TO BRING AN END TO THE TIMES OF THE GENTILES (Lk. 21:24; Rom. 11:25; Zech. 14:4-11);

12. TO POSSESS THE EARTH (Ps. 2; Rev. 11:15);

13. TO EVANGELIZE THE WORLD (Isa. 2:1-4; 11:9; 52:7; 66:19-24; Zech. 8:23; 10:1; 14:16-21; Mal. 1:11);

14. TO MAKE A RESTORATION OF ALL THINGS (Acts 3:19-21);

15. TO BIND SATAN AND HIS ANGELS (Rev. 20:1-10; Isa. 24:21-23);

16. TO PUNISH SIN AND UNRIGHTEOUSNESS (Isa. 26:21; 27:1; Rev. 11:18);

17. TO ENTER INTO THE BATTLE OF ARMAGEDDON AND DEFEAT THE ENEMY (Rev. 19:11-21);

18. TO ESTABLISH A GODLY GOVERNMENT (Ps. 2; Isa. 2:1-4; Dan. 2:44 45; Rev., Chpt. 20);

19. TO FULFILL HIS COVENANTS WITH ABRAHAM AND DAVID (Gen., Chpts. 12; 15; 18; II Sam., Chpt. 7); AND,

20. TO BRING HEALING (Isa. 32:1-5; 35:5).

TIME OF HIS COMING

At this point in time we cannot say exactly *when* Christ will return. But we know that (1) according to Matthew 24:34 all the signs of His Coming will be fulfilled in one generation and (2) according to Matthew 24:36 the exact date of His Coming is unknown. And we also do know that His Coming will mark the timing of, or coincide with, certain other events. Therefore, we can say, from Scripture, that . . .

1. HE WILL COME AT THE END OF THE TRIBULATION.

"Immediately after the tribulation of those days shall the sun be darkened, and the moon shall not give her light, and the stars shall fall from Heaven, and the powers of the Heavens shall be shaken:

"And then shall appear the sign of the Son of Man in Heaven" (Mat. 24:29-30).

2. HE WILL COME AFTER THE REIGN OF THE ANTI-CHRIST.

"Then shall that Wicked be revealed, whom the Lord shall consume with the spirit of His Mouth, and shall destroy with the brightness of His Coming" (II Thess. 2:8).

3. HE WILL COME IN DAYS LIKE LOT'S AND NOAH'S.

"But as the days of Noah were, so shall also the coming of the Son of Man be" (Mat. 24:37).

4. HE WILL COME WHEN JERUSALEM IS SURROUNDED BY ARMIES.

"When you shall see Jerusalem compassed with armies . . . then shall they see the Son of Man coming in a cloud with Power and great Glory" (Lk. 21:20, 27).

5. HE WILL COME WHEN THE 10 KINGDOMS ARE FORMED INSIDE THE OLD ROMAN EMPIRE.

"And in the days of these kings shall the God of Heaven set up a Kingdom, which shall never be destroyed" (Dan. 2:44-45).

6. HE WILL COME WHEN THE GOSPEL IS PREACHED IN ALL THE WORLD.

"And this Gospel of the Kingdom shall be preached in all the world for a witness unto all nations; and then shall the end come" (Mat. 24:14).

7. HE WILL COME IN SUCH AN HOUR AS YOU THINK NOT.

"Therefore be ye also ready: for in such an hour as you think not the Son of Man comes" (Mat. 24:44).

8. HE WILL COME WHEN THE POWERS OF HEAVEN ARE SHAKEN.

"The stars of Heaven shall fall, and the powers that are in Heaven shall be shaken.
"And then shall they see the Son of Man coming in the clouds with great Power and Glory" (Mk. 13:25-26).

When the Antichrist has conquered the 10 kingdoms inside the Old Roman Empire, and by them have conquered other nations, then it will be time for the world to be thinking *"peace and safety."*

"For yourselves know perfectly that the Day of the Lord so comes as a thief in the night.
"For when they shall say, Peace and safety; then SUDDEN destruction comes upon them . . . and they shall not escape" (I Thess. 5:2-3).

The Antichrist will think that making an end of Israel will solve all his problems and end all wars. But the Lord will come suddenly to defend the Holy City and the Holy People and to destroy her enemy.

SIGNS OF HIS COMING

The Second Coming of Christ, not the Rapture, is referred to in Matthew, Chapter 24; Mark, Chapter 13; and, Luke, Chapter 21. Other than the signs of the culmination of events leading up to the Great Tribulation and the Endtimes (such as we see all around us), there are no events that must first occur before the Rapture of the Church, for it could take place at any moment. All of these signs of the coming of Jesus Christ point to the

Second Coming *after* the Tribulation.

These signs are as follows:

1. DECEPTION (Mat. 24:4-5, 11, 24);

2. FALSE CHRISTS (Mat. 24:5, 23-26);

3. WARS AND RUMORS OF WAR (Mat. 24:6-7);

4. FAMINE (Mat. 24:7; Rev. 6:5-6);

5. PESTILENCE (Mat. 24:7; Rev. 6:8);

6. EARTHQUAKES (Mat. 24:7; Rev. 6:12-17);

7. ANTI-SEMITISM (Mat. 24:9; Mk. 13:9, 13);

8. HATRED (Mat. 24:10-13; II Tim. 3:1-9);

9. FALSE PROPHETS (Mat. 24:11, 24; Rev., Chpt. 13);

10. LAWLESSNESS (Mat. 24:12);

11. EVANGELIZATION (Mat. 24:14);

12. GREAT TRIBULATION (Mat. 24:21; Rev., Chpts. 12 through 19);

13. ANARCHY AND UNREST (Lk. 21:9; II Tim. 3:1-5);

14. SIGNS AND WONDERS (Lk. 21:11; Rev., Chpts. 6 through 16);

15. MARTYRDOM (Mat. 24:9, 22; Dan. 7:21; 12:10; Rev. 7:9-17);

16. IMMORTALITY (Mat. 24:38; Lk. 17:27);

17. SPIRITUAL APATHY (Mat. 24:39);

18. LASCIVIOUSNESS (Mat. 24:38; Lk. 17:28; 21:34);

19. TEN KINGDOMS (Dan. 2:44-45);

20. ANTICHRIST (II Thess. 2:3);

21. ABOMINATION OF DESOLATION (Mat. 24:15; Dan. 9:27);

22. JEWISH TEMPLE (Mat. 24:15, 26; Rev. 11:1-2);

23. NATIONAL ISRAEL (Mat. 24:9, 15-26; Ezek., Chpt. 37; Dan. 9:27);

24. SATANIC ACTIVITY (Mat. 24:24; Rev., Chpts. 13 through 19); AND,

25. FEAR (Lk. 21:26).

CONTRAST BETWEEN THE RAPTURE AND THE SECOND COMING

The Greek *parousia*, meaning the Personal, visible Presence or Appearing — *"coming"* — of Christ, may refer to either of two appearings: (1) the Rapture, the Personal Coming in the air, not to the Earth, *for* the Saints (I Thess. 2:19; 3:13; 4:13-17; 5:23; I Cor. 15:23, 51-58; II Thess. 2:1, 7-8; James 5:7-8; I Jn. 2:28; Jn. 14:1-3) or (2) the Second Coming of Christ, to the Earth, *with* the Saints, to reign (Mat. 24:3, 27-51; 25:31-46; Jude, Vss. 14-15; Rev. 19:11-21; Zech., Chpt. 14).

We should not confuse these two comings. The Scriptures that refer to one do not refer to the other. They are two distinct comings in Scripture, and not one Biblical Passage confuses the two.

The Rapture is the First Coming and occurs before the Tribulation. At that time Christ will not come to Earth. He will meet the Saints in the air. He will take the Saints back to Heaven and present them to the Father. They will remain in Heaven during the Great Tribulation. In Heaven they will stand before the Judgment of Rewards and eat the Marriage Supper of the Lamb.

The Second Coming takes place seven years after the Rapture. At that time Christ will come to the Earth. He will bring the Saints with Him. He will fight the armies of the Antichrist and set up the Millennial Kingdom. This event cannot take place until after the events of Revelation, Chapters 4 through 19 are fulfilled.

REFERENCES TO THE RAPTURE

"Pray always, that you may be accounted worthy to escape all these things that shall come to pass, and to stand before the Son of Man" (Lk. 21:36).

"In my Father's House are many mansions . . . I go to prepare a place for you.

"And if I go and prepare a place for you, I will come again, and receive you unto Myself; that where I am, there you may be also" (Jn. 14:1-3).

"We shall not all sleep, but we shall all be changed,

"In a moment, in the twinkling of an eye, at the last trump: for the trumpet shall sound, and the dead shall be raised incorruptible, and we shall be changed" (I Cor. 15:51-52).

"Even as Christ also loved the Church, and gave Himself for it;

"That He might sanctify and cleanse it with the washing of water by the Word,

"That He might present it to Himself a glorious Church, not having spot, or wrinkle, or any such thing; but that it should be Holy and without blemish" (Eph. 5:25-27).

"For our conversation is in Heaven; from whence also we look for the Saviour, the Lord Jesus Christ:

"Who shall change our vile body, that it may be fashioned like unto His Glorious Body, according to the working whereby He is able even to subdue all things unto Himself" (Phil. 3:20-21).

"For we know that if our earthly house of this Tabernacle were dissolved, we have a building of God, an house not made with hands, eternal in the Heavens.

"For in this we groan, earnestly desiring to be clothed upon with our house which is from Heaven:

"We are confident, I say, and willing rather to be absent from the body, and to be present with the Lord" (II Cor. 5:1- 8).

"For the Lord Himself shall descend from Heaven with a shout, with the voice of the Archangel, and with the Trump of God: and the dead in Christ shall rise first:

"Then we which are alive and remain shall be caught up together with them in the clouds, to meet the Lord in the air: and so shall we ever be with the Lord" (I Thess. 4:16-17).

"And the very God of Peace Sanctify you wholly; and I pray God your whole spirit and soul and body be preserved blameless unto the coming of our Lord Jesus Christ" (I Thess. 5:23).

"Now we beseech you, Brethren, by the coming of our Lord Jesus Christ, and by our gathering together unto Him" (II Thess. 2:1).

"When Christ, Who is our life, shall appear, then shall you also appear with Him in Glory" (Col. 3:4).

"And now, little children, abide in Him; that, when He shall appear, we may have confidence, and not be ashamed before Him at His Coming" (I Jn. 2:28).

"And when the Chief Shepherd shall appear, you shall receive a crown of glory that fades not away" (I Pet. 5:4).

SELF-HELP STUDY NOTES

141

REFERENCES TO THE SECOND COMING

"And in the days of these kings shall the God of Heaven set up a Kingdom, which shall never be destroyed" (Dan. 2:44-45).

"And, behold, One like the Son of Man came with the clouds of Heaven" (Dan. 7:13-14).

"And His Feet shall stand in that day upon the Mount of Olives, which is before Jerusalem on the east, and the Mount of Olives shall cleave in the midst thereof toward the east and toward the west, and there shall be a very great valley; and half of the mountain shall remove toward the north, and half of it toward the south" (Zech. 14:4).

"Immediately after the Tribulation of those days shall the sun be darkened, and the moon shall not give her light, and the stars shall fall from Heaven, and the powers of the Heavens shall be shaken:

"And then shall appear the sign of the Son of Man in Heaven: and then shall all the tribes of the Earth mourn, and they shall see the Son of Man coming in the clouds of Heaven with Power and great Glory" (Mat. 24:29-30).

"The Son of Man shall come in His Glory, and all the Holy Angels with Him, then shall He sit upon the Throne of His Glory" (Mat. 25:31).

"The Lord Jesus shall be revealed from Heaven with His mighty Angels,

"In flaming fire taking vengeance on them who know not God, and who obey not the Gospel of our Lord Jesus Christ:

"Who shall be punished with everlasting destruction . . .

"When He shall come to be glorified in His Saints, and to be admired in all them who believe" (II Thess. 1:7-10).

"Then shall that Wicked be revealed, whom the Lord shall consume with the Spirit of His Mouth, and shall destroy with the Brightness of His Coming" (II Thess. 2:8).

"Behold, the Lord comes with ten thousands of His Saints,

"To execute Judgment upon all, and to convince all who are ungodly among them of all their ungodly deeds which they have ungodly committed" (Jude, Vss. 14-15).

"For the day of vengeance is in My Heart, and the year of

My Redeemed is come.

"And I looked, and there was none to help; and I wondered that there was none to uphold: therefore My Own Arm brought Salvation unto Me" (Isa. 63:4-5).

"The LORD also shall roar out of Zion, and utter His Voice from Jerusalem; and the Heavens and the Earth shall shake: but the LORD will be the Hope of His People" (Joel 3:16).

"Behold, He comes with clouds; and every eye shall see Him, and they also which pierced Him: and all kindreds of the Earth shall wail because of Him. Even so, Amen" (Rev. 1:7).

"And I saw Heaven opened, and behold a white horse; and He Who sat upon him was called Faithful and True, and in Righteousness He does judge and make war . . .

"And the armies which were in Heaven followed Him upon white horses, clothed in fine linen, white and clean" (Rev. 19:11-21).

TRUMP OF GOD

The expression *"the Trump of God"* found in I Thessalonians 4:16-17 has no connection with the *"Trumpet Judgments"* of Revelation, Chapters 11 through 13. One *"Trump of God"* sounds at the Rapture of the Church before the Tribulation. Another *"trumpet"* sounds at the rapture of the Man Child in the middle of the Tribulation. The first is the *"Trump of God"*; the second, the trumpet of the Angel. The first will herald an event that will take place suddenly; the second, events that will take place over a period of days.

A trumpet is mentioned as sounding at both the Rapture (I Cor. 15:52; I Thess. 4:16-17) and the Second Coming (Zech. 9:14; Mat. 24:31). The Bible never says the trumpet will be blown by the Angel Gabriel. It does say in Zechariah 9:14 that the Lord God Himself will blow the trumpet!

PROPHECIES OF THE SECOND COMING

We read in the Word of God of Patriarchs, Kings, Prophets, Songwriters, Apostles, Law-Givers, Angels, even Jesus Himself foretelling the great event we know as the Second Coming of Christ.

The Patriarch Jacob testified of the Second Coming when he said:

"The sceptre shall not depart from Judah, nor a Law-Giver

from between His Feet, until Shiloh come; and unto Him shall the gathering of the people be" (Gen. 49:10).

Balaam, who could not curse what God had blessed, said of Him:

"There shall come a Star out of Jacob, and a Sceptre shall rise out of Israel, and shall smite the corners of Moab, and destroy all the children of Sheth.

"Out of Jacob shall come He Who shall have dominion, and shall destroy him who remains of the city" (Num. 24:17, 19).

Enoch, the seventh from Adam, prophesied:

"Behold, the Lord comes with ten thousands of His Saints" (Jude, Vs. 14).

Job, the great sufferer, held fast to his Faith:

"For I know that my Redeemer lives, and that He shall stand at the latter day upon the Earth" (Job 19:25).

King David, the sweet singer of Israel, expressed:

"He shall come down like rain upon the mown grass . . . He shall have dominion also from sea to sea, and from the river unto the ends of the Earth" (Ps. 72:6-8).

Isaiah said:

"And the Redeemer shall come to Zion" (Isa. 59:20).

Daniel said:

"And, behold, One like the Son of Man came with the clouds of Heaven. . . .

"And there was given Him dominion, and Glory, and a Kingdom . . . His dominion is an everlasting dominion, which shall not pass away" (Dan. 7:13-14).

Micah prophesied:

"Behold, the LORD comes forth out of His place, and will

come down, and tread upon the high places of the Earth.

"And the mountains shall be molten under Him, and the valleys shall be cleft, as wax before the fire, and as the waters that are poured down a steep place" (Mic. 1:3-4).

Zechariah foretold:

"And His Feet shall stand in that day upon the Mount of Olives. . . .
"And the LORD shall be King over all the Earth" (Zech. 14:4, 9).

Malachi foresaw:

"But who may abide the day of His Coming? and who shall stand when He appears? for He is like a refiner's fire, and like fullers' soap.
"And He shall sit as a Refiner and Purifier of silver. . . .
"But unto you who fear My Name shall the Sun of Righteousness arise with healing in His Wings" (Mal. 3:2-3; 4:2).

Jesus Himself testified:

"For the Son of Man shall come in the Glory of His Father with His Angels; and then He shall reward every man according to his works" (Mat. 16:27).

"And then shall appear the sign of the Son of Man in Heaven: and then shall all the tribes of the Earth mourn, and they shall see the Son of Man coming in the clouds of Heaven with Power and great Glory.
"And He shall send His Angels with a great sound of a trumpet, and they shall gather together His Elect from the four winds, from one end of Heaven to the other" (Mat. 24:30-31).

"Hereafter shall you see the Son of Man sitting on the Right Hand of Power, and coming in the clouds of Heaven" (Mat. 26:64).

"You have heard how I said unto you, I go away, and come again unto you. . . .
"And now I have told you before it come to pass, that, when it is come to pass, you might believe" (Jn. 14:28-29).

145

The Angel testified:

"This same Jesus, which is taken up from you into Heaven, shall so come in like manner as you have seen Him go into Heaven" (Acts 1:11).

James, the brother of our Lord and leader of the Early Church, affirmed:

"Simeon has declared how God at the first did visit the Gentiles, to take out of them a people for His Name.
"And to this agree the words of the Prophets; as it is written,
"After this I will return, and will build again the Tabernacle of David" (Acts. 15:14-16).

Paul the Apostle wrote to Timothy:

"I give you charge in the sight of God, who quickens all things . . .
"That you keep this Commandment without spot, unrebukeable, until the appearing of our Lord Jesus Christ:
"Which in His times He shall show, Who is the Blessed and only Potentate, the King of kings, and Lord of lords;
"Who only has immortality, dwelling in the Light which no man can approach unto; Whom no man has seen, nor can see" (I Tim. 6:13-16).

"I charge you therefore before God, and the Lord Jesus Christ, Who shall judge the quick and the dead at His Appearing and His Kingdom;
"Henceforth there is laid up for me a Crown of Righteousness, which the Lord, the Righteous Judge, shall give me at that day: and not to me only, but unto all them also who love His Appearing" (II Tim. 4:1, 8).

The Apostle Peter related:

"We have not followed cunningly devised fables, when we made known unto you the Power and Coming of our Lord Jesus Christ, but were eyewitnesses of His Majesty.
"There shall come in the last days scoffers, walking after their own lusts, And saying, Where is the Promise of His

Coming? for since the fathers fell asleep, all things continue as they were from the beginning of the Creation.

"The Lord is not slack concerning His Promise, as some men count slackness; but is longsuffering to us-ward, not willing that any should perish, but that all should come to Repentance" (II Pet. 1:16; 3:3-4, 9).

Although we cannot know the day or the hour of Christ's coming again, we can know the times and the seasons. We do know the Second Coming will be at least seven years after the Rapture and just prior to the 1,000-year Reign of Christ on Earth. Jesus used the fig tree as an illustration, saying that when the branch is tender and puts forth leaves, we know summer is near. So, in like manner, when we see all these things begin to come to pass, we can know that it is time for His Return (read Mk. 13:28-29).

Current world events point to the Endtime. Signs indicate the nearness of the Rapture, the Tribulation, Armageddon, the Second Coming. Jesus said that *"generation"* or *"race"* or *"lineage"* would not pass away until *"all"* these things would be fulfilled (Mk. 13:30-33). Ever since the restoration of Israel to the Promised Land in 1948, we have witnessed that *"generation."* Surely, of all the epochs of history *this* is the time to be looking, working, and waiting for His Return!

Chapter 5

The Millennium

CHAPTER FIVE

THE MILLENNIUM

The 1,000-year Reign will begin when the Lord Jesus Christ returns to Earth with all the Saints, interrupting the Battle of Armageddon, sets His Feet upon the Mount of Olives, and establishes His Kingdom in the Holy City, Jerusalem, Israel.

We know that, first, Satan must be bound (Rev. 20:1-10), for we read in Revelation 20:3 that Satan will be bound during the Millennium. Also, Revelation 20:4 tells us that the Great Tribulation Martyrs will have a part in the First Resurrection, which takes place before the 1,000 years and includes all the different companies of the redeemed and every individual Saved — from Adam to the binding of Satan. This Verse also implies that the Tribulation Saints will be the last redeemed company resurrected and translated. The First Resurrection will end with the rapture of the two witnesses and this company.

The Millennial Kingdom will be a literal kingdom, with the Lord Jesus Christ reigning in Jerusalem. Just as all preceding kingdoms have been literal, so this one will be literal as well (Isa. 9:6-7; Dan. 2:44-45; 7:13; Zech., Chpt. 14; Rev. 17:8-18).

PROMISE OF AN EVERLASTING KINGDOM

Both the Abrahamic Covenant and the Davidic Covenant promised that Israel would have an *everlasting earthly kingdom* through which all of the families of the Earth would be blessed (Gen. 12:1-3; 13:14-17; 17:6-8; II Sam. 7:8-17; Ps. 89:3-4, 20-37).

That is the reason the Jews were looking for a King as their Messiah, the Prince of the house of David. They blindly overlooked the Prophecies concerning His First Advent as a suffering Saviour, because there are so many more Prophecies of His Second Advent as a reigning King!

From Genesis to Malachi there is a note of praise, as Law-Giver and Historian, Psalmist and Prophet constantly referring to the Kingdom Age, when the Messiah will reign.

From Matthew to Revelation the hope continues as John the Baptist, the Lord Jesus Christ, and all of the Apostles preach the Gospel of the Kingdom. The Prophecy went forth in the Early Church that . . .

"God at the first did visit the Gentiles, to take out of them a people for His Name . . .

"After this I will return, and will build again the Tabernacle of David, which is fallen down; and I will build again the ruins thereof, and I will set it up:

"That the residue of men might seek after the Lord, and all the Gentiles, upon whom My Name is called, saith the Lord, Who does all these things" (Acts 15:14-17).

This everlasting Kingdom will be established during the Millennium.

NAMES FOR THE MILLENNIUM

Our English word *"millennium"* does not appear in the Bible. *"Millennium"* comes from two Latin words, *mille*, meaning *"thousand,"* and *annum*, meaning *"years"*; hence 1,000 years.

The Doctrine of the Millennial Reign is strongly substantiated in Scripture. It is referred to as . . .

1. THE 1,000-YEAR REIGN OF CHRIST (Rev. 20:4, 6);

2. THE DISPENSATION OF THE FULNESS OF TIME (Eph. 1:10);

3. THE DAY OF THE LORD (Isa. 2:12; 13:6, 9; 34:8, Joel 2:1, 11, 31; 3:14; Zech. 14:1-9);

4. THAT DAY (Ezek. 39:22; 48:35; Hos. 2:18; Zech. 12:8-11; 13:1; Mal. 3:17);

5. THE AGE TO COME (Mat. 12:32; Mk. 10:30; Lk. 18:30; Eph. 1:21; 2:7);

6. THE KINGDOM OF CHRIST AND OF GOD (Eph. 5:5; Mat. 20:21; II Tim. 4:1; Jn. 18:28-37; I Cor. 15:24-28; Dan. 7:13-14; Rev. 11:15);

7. THE KINGDOM OF GOD (Mk. 14:25; Lk. 10:11; 22:14-18);

8. THE KINGDOM OF HEAVEN (Mat. 7:21; 8:11; 10:7);

9. THE REGENERATION (Mat. 19:28);

10. THE TIMES OF THE RESTITUTION OF ALL THINGS (Acts 3:20-21);

11. THE CONSOLATION OF ISRAEL (Lk. 2:25);

12. THE REDEMPTION IN JERUSALEM (Lk. 2:38);

13. THE TIMES OF REFRESHING (Acts 3:19); AND,

14. THE KINGDOM OF THEIR FATHER (Mat. 13:43).

Many Verses in the Old Testament speak of Israel's full restoration to the Promised Land. But the Scriptures also speak of a spiritual restoration as well.

>*"Behold, the days come, saith the Lord, when I will make a New Covenant with the House of Israel and with the House of Judah:*
>
>*"Not according to the Covenant that I made with their fathers in the day when I took them by the hand to lead them out of the land of Egypt; because they continued not in My Covenant, and I regarded them not, says the Lord.*
>
>*"For this is the Covenant that I will make with the House of Israel after those days, saith the Lord; I WILL PUT MY LAWS INTO THEIR MIND, AND WRITE THEM IN THEIR HEARTS: AND I WILL BE TO THEM A GOD, AND THEY SHALL BE TO ME A PEOPLE:*
>
>*"And they shall not teach every man his neighbour, and every man his brother, saying, Know the Lord: for all shall know Me, from the least to the greatest.*
>
>*"For I will be merciful to their unrighteousness, and their sins and their iniquities will I remember no more"* (Heb. 8:8-12).

What a Prophecy! The Apostle Paul elsewhere expounded:

>*"For I would not, Brethren, that you should be ignorant of this mystery . . . that blindness in part is happened to Israel, until the fulness of the Gentiles be come in.*
>
>*"And so ALL ISRAEL SHALL BE SAVED"* (Rom. 11:25-26).

At the end of the Great Tribulation Period, when the godless military hordes of the Antichrist and his alliance are coming against the Holy Land and to the Holy People, to exterminate them from the face of the Earth, the Lord Jesus Christ will appear in the skies, with the Armies of Heaven, to defend His chosen People and to put an end to the invading armies of the Antichrist.

At this point the national Salvation of the Holy People will take place.

>*"And it shall come to pass in that day, that I will seek to destroy all the nations that come against Jerusalem.*

"And I will pour upon the house of David and upon the inhabitants of Jerusalem, the Spirit of Grace and of Supplications: and THEY SHALL LOOK UPON ME WHOM THEY HAVE PIERCED, AND THEY SHALL MOURN FOR HIM, AS ONE MOURNS FOR HIS ONLY SON, AND SHALL BE IN BITTERNESS FOR HIM, AS ONE THAT IS IN BITTERNESS FOR HIS FIRSTBORN.

"In that day there shall be a FOUNTAIN OPENED TO THE HOUSE OF DAVID AND TO THE INHABITANTS OF JERUSALEM FOR SIN AND FOR UNCLEANNESS.

". . . they shall call on My Name, and I will hear them: I will say, It is My People: and they shall say, The LORD is my God" (Zech. 12:9-10; 13:1, 9).

BINDING OF SATAN

After Israel's national repentance, Satan will be bound for 1,000 years.

"And I saw an Angel come down from Heaven, having the key of the bottomless pit and a great chain in his hand.

"AND HE LAID HOLD ON THE DRAGON, THAT OLD SERPENT, WHICH IS THE DEVIL, AND SATAN, AND BOUND HIM A THOUSAND YEARS,

"And cast him into the bottomless pit, and shut him up, and set a seal upon him, that he should deceive the nations no more, till the thousand years should be fulfilled: and after that he must be loosed a little season" (Rev. 20:1-3).

After the Battle of Armageddon, upon the initiation of the Millennial Reign, Satan will be bound in chains and cast into the bottomless pit. No human being ever goes to the bottomless pit. The pit is not the Lake of Fire (gehenna), where Satan — along with wicked men, demons, fallen angels, and all rebellious creatures — will finally be sentenced to eternal torment.

The object of this binding and imprisonment of Satan and his legions will be the temporary end of temptation and deception. At the end of the Millennium he will be loosed for a little season.

It has been taught erroneously that Satan was bound at the Baptism and Temptation of Jesus (Mat. 3:13 through 4:11) and this is indicated by Jesus' power to cast out devils. However, the Apostle Peter warned us:

"Your adversary the Devil, as a roaring lion, WALKS ABOUT, seeking whom he may devour" (I Pet. 5:8).

This shows us that Satan has not been bound and that he is much active on Planet Earth.

If there was ever a time when Satan was loose, active, and powerful in human affairs, that time is now, in this present day. We are living in days of moral decline, falsehood, lies, deception, and greed. And yet, thank God, we are simultaneously experiencing seasons of great Revival!

Most liberal Bible Colleges and Seminaries scoff at such a thing as a literal, personal Devil or a literal, burning Hell. Humanist teaching mixed with liberal theology has pervaded the intellectual thinking of our nation for the past century, teaching that within every man there is a spark of the divine, and that all we have to do to ignite it is to fan the embers with education. Then we will become little gods who will usher in a utopia right here on Earth.

Such things as Judgment and Righteousness are a thing of the past. Reverence scarcely exists anymore. Oaths and pledges are no longer binding. Moral guilt and Repentance are, by and large, trampled underfoot beneath the weight of greed, lust, and deified flesh.

People pride themselves in falsehoods and outright lies, which they speak and print and gloat over, as if they were an end in themselves. And yet, some teachers would have us to believe that Satan is already bound!

Satan's activities are increasing daily as he sees his end approaching, for he knows his time is short.

Satan promises freedom without responsibility, church membership without dues, creeds and dogmas without life, religion without Christ (or the Blood), ecumenicism without absolutes, experience without a corresponding change of heart and life, easy-believism that leads the wary and unsuspecting and dupes into a false hope, entertainment instead of commitment, platitudes instead of Prophecy, and prestige instead of Power.

And yet Satan is bound?

"BE NOT DECEIVED; GOD IS NOT MOCKED" (Gal. 6:7).

No, Satan is not bound *now*, but praise God, he will be *someday!*

REIGNING THRONES

The Bible mentions two future Resurrections for mankind. The *"first resurrection"* (Rev. 20:5) is a Resurrection of the Righteous dead, which will take place *before* the Millennium. It will include all of the different companies of the redeemed, Saved during each period of human history. The Great Tribulation Saints will be the last company resurrected and translated. All of these will have a part in the First Resurrection, which is the Resurrection of the living Saints who will reign with Christ during the 1,000 years.

The wicked dead will have no part in the First Resurrection, because they will not be resurrected until *after* the Millennium (Rev. 20:5). This is the *"second resurrection,"* which will include all of the wicked dead from each period of human history, including the Millennium. Their souls will remain in Hell until the end of the Millennium, when they will be resurrected to stand before the Great White Throne Judgment (Rev. 20:11-15).

Those who have a part in the First Resurrection will be pronounced *"blessed and holy,"* but those who have a part in the Second Resurrection will have their part in the Lake of Fire (Rev. 20:15; 21:8).

> *"I saw Thrones, and they sat upon them, and Judgment was given unto them: and I saw the souls of them who were beheaded for the witness of Jesus, and for the Word of God, and which had not worshipped the Beast, neither his image, neither had received his mark upon their foreheads, or in their hands; AND THEY LIVED AND REIGNED WITH CHRIST A THOUSAND YEARS"* (Rev. 20:4).

We see in this Verse that there are thrones and occupants of thrones, which are the Great Tribulation Martyrs. They, with other redeemed people, will rule and reign as . . .

"Kings and Priests" (Rev. 5:10).

All the Saints that have ever lived will be judged and rewarded according to the deeds done in the body, and will be given places of rulership according to their rewards — not according to the company of redeemed of which they are a part or according to the age in which they lived.

For example, King David will have a greater rulership than any one of the Apostles. He will be King over all Israel, while the Apostles will have only one Tribe each. Some of the Old Testament Saints did much more for God and had more Power than some New Testament Saints, and they will be given authority commensurate with what they did while on Earth (Ps. 149:5-9; Rom. 8:17; I Cor. 4:8; Eph. 2:17; II Thess. 1:4-7; II Tim. 2:12).

The government will be not a monarchy, democracy, or autocracy, but a theocracy, meaning that God Himself will be its Head. God will reign through the Lord Jesus Christ (Mat. 25:31-46; Lk. 1:32-35; Rev. 11:15), through King David, who will actually rule the Nation of Israel (Jer. 30:9; Ezek. 34:24; Hos. 3:4-5), and through the redeemed Saints (Rev. 5:10).

The Kingdom will be a literal Kingdom, just like any other kingdom on Earth. Before the era of the Prophet Daniel, there had been two earthly kingdoms: Egypt and Assyria. Daniel and Revelation both mention six kingdoms: Babylon, Medo-Persia, Greece, Rome, Revised Rome, and Revised Greece. The Millennial Kingdom will be the ninth earthly kingdom (Isa. 9:6-7; Dan. 2:44-45; 7:13-14, 17-27; Zech., Chpt. 14; Rev. 17:8-18).

After the Battle of Armageddon and the Return of Jesus Christ, there will be many persons left of all nations of the Earth. These will go up from year to year to worship the Lord of Hosts and to keep the Feast of Tabernacles. It is these people and their children who will populate the Earth during the Millennium.

> *"And it shall come to pass, that every one who is left of all the nations which came against Jerusalem shall even go up from year to year to worship the King, the LORD of Hosts, and to keep the Feast of Tabernacles"* (Zech. 14:16).

> *"And it shall come to pass in the last days, that the mountain of the LORD's house shall be established in the top of the mountains, and shall be exalted above the hills; and all nations shall flow unto it.*
> *"And many people shall go and say, Come ye, and let us go up to the mountain of the LORD, to the House of the God of Jacob; and He will teach us of His Ways, and we will walk in His Paths: for out of Zion shall go forth the Law, and the Word of the LORD from Jerusalem"* (Isa. 2:2-3).

The Millennial Kingdom will be worldwide and will forever increase in every respect just as every other kingdom, except that it will not have sin and rebellion (Ps. 72:8; Isa. 9:6-7; Dan. 7:13-14; Zech. 9:10; Rev. 11:15).

Earthly nations and natural peoples will continue as such in the Kingdom forever and ever. All people, nations, and languages will serve the Lord.

> *"His dominion is an everlasting dominion, which shall not pass away, and His Kingdom . . . shall not be destroyed"* (Dan. 7:14).

HOLINESS UNTO THE LORD

Every industry in America, every high school, every university, every club, every organization, every power structure has its logo. It is even common practice among nations of the world to place an imprint on their products: *"Made in USA," "Made in Japan," "Made in Hong Kong."* Ancient peoples had an inscription to symbolize their nation. Relics dug up in Baghdad bear the egotistical inscription: *"Nebuchadnezzar, son of Nabopolassar, king of Babylon."*

In the Millennium things will be much the same, except there will be no national identity, such as USA, Japan, Hong Kong. There will be one Government, one Kingdom, one King. All manufactured goods will bear His Inscription, *"HOLINESS UNTO THE LORD."*

> *"In that day shall there be upon the bells of the horses, HOLINESS UNTO THE LORD; and the pots in the LORD'S house shall be like the bowls before the Altar.*
> *"Yea, every pot in Jerusalem and in Judah shall be HOLINESS UNTO THE LORD OF HOSTS"* (Zech. 14:20-21).

> *"And her merchandise and her hire shall be HOLINESS TO THE LORD: it shall not be treasured nor laid up; for her merchandise shall be for them who dwell before the LORD, to eat sufficiently, and for durable clothing"* (Isa. 23:18).

Compare Exodus 28:36; 39:22-31.

The identifying imprint, HOLINESS UNTO THE LORD, will spread throughout the entire Earth. For the first time in human history, Holiness will be not only a beautiful life, but also a popular word. Yes, it will be the Divine Logo, true, but, more important, it will be an indelible imprint on the life of countless multitudes of people who love and worship King Jesus!

People have a tendency to shape their life after that which is placed before them. The Old Testament taught this principle by requiring children to wear bracelets and headbands with the Law, and the Commandments, inscribed on them. Also, the Commandments were placed on the doorposts and other areas so that they might be kept uppermost — fresh — in the mind of the people.

In Deuteronomy 5:6-21 we have a repetition of the Ten Commandments. A Chapter later we have the Word of the Lord:

> *"And these words, which I command you this day, shall be in your heart.*
> *"And you shall bind them for a sign upon your hand, and they shall be as frontlets between your eyes.*
> *"And you shall write them upon the posts of your house, and on your gates"* (Deut. 6:6, 8-9).

Our whole advertisement system today is based on this same principle: lay it before the people's eyes and implant the thought in their mind by constant bombardment! So, HOLINESS UNTO THE LORD will be seen throughout the Millennial Kingdom as a constant reminder.

LAWS OF THE KINGDOM

Those who have been truly Born-Again and fully committed to the Lord, and who have fellowship with God during the 1,000 years, will not rebel, but there will be sinners alive during the Millennium. For this reason the Kingdom will have laws and regulations.

The sinners will be people who have survived the Tribulation, but who did not take the mark of the Beast. They will not be Saved when the Millennium begins, but will be allowed to live through it. They will not be changed by the transforming Power of the Cross. Some of these may even be executed because of committing sins worthy of the death penalty.

"The Spirit of Knowledge and of the Fear of the LORD;

"And shall make Him of quick understanding in the Fear of the LORD: and He shall not judge after the sight of His Eyes, neither reprove after the hearing of His Ears:

"But with Righteousness shall He judge the poor, and reprove with equity for the meek of the Earth: and He shall smite the Earth with the rod of His Mouth, and with the breath of His Lips shall He slay the wicked.

"And Righteousness shall be the girdle of His Loins, and Faithfulness the girdle of His Reins" (Isa. 11:2-5).

"There shall be no more thence an infant of days, nor an old man who has not filled his days: for the child shall die an hundred years old; but the sinner being an hundred years old shall be accursed.

"And they shall build houses, and inhabit them; and they shall plant vineyards, and eat the fruit of them.

"They shall not build, and another inhabit; they shall not plant, and another eat: for as the days of a tree are the days of My People, and My Elect shall long enjoy the work of their hands" (Isa. 65:20-22).

There will be Laws to govern and to keep order. Quick action will be instituted for refusal to follow the Rules and Laws of God. Even though the Millennium will be a Righteous Reign, and even though Satan will be bound for 1,000 years, man still will be depraved and hopelessly sinful without giving his heart to the Lord Jesus Christ and finding remission of sin. Multitudes of people will be Saved, healed, and delivered during this glorious Reign of Jesus Christ!

The Laws of the Kingdom will include those given to Israel as an eternal standard of Holiness (Isa. 2:2-4; Mic. 4:1-2; Ezek. 40:1 through 48:35) and the Laws of the New Covenant given by Christ. The terms of the Gospel will apply to everyone, although some of the Laws will apply only to Israel in the Promised Land. Some of Israel's feasts will be required of all nationalities. If these do not participate, God will withdraw His Providence from them.

"And it shall come to pass, that every one who is left of all the nations which came against Jerusalem shall even go up from year to year to worship the King, the LORD of Hosts, and to keep the Feast of Tabernacles.

"And it shall be, that whoso will not come up of all the families of the Earth unto Jerusalem to worship the King, the LORD of Hosts, even upon them shall be no rain.

"And if the family of Egypt go not up, and come not, who have no rain; there shall be the plague, wherewith the LORD will smite the heathen who come not up to keep the Feast of Tabernacles.

"This shall be the punishment of Egypt, and the punishment of all nations that come not up to keep the Feast of Tabernacles" (Zech. 14:16-19).

There will be no lengthy court proceedings, appeals, and injustice, for God Himself will be the final Judge.

THE REIGNING KING

Presently the rule of the Earth is in the hands of the Devil, under his influence, and not under the command of the Saints. But during the Millennium, the rule of the Earth will be exclusively in the Hands of the Lord of lords and His Saints with Him.

Now we can only beseech men to come to Christ.

"God . . . has reconciled us to Himself by Jesus Christ, and has given to us the Ministry of Reconciliation;

"To wit, that God was in Christ, reconciling the world

unto Himself . . . and has committed unto us the Word of Reconciliation.

"Now then we are Ambassadors for Christ, as though God did beseech you by us: we pray you in Christ's stead, be you reconciled to God" (II Cor. 5:18-20).

But in that day men will be compelled to take the instructions given to them and to serve the Lord with fear and to rejoice with trembling:

"Serve the LORD with fear, and rejoice with trembling.
"Kiss the Son (that is, worship Him and give Him homage), *lest He be angry, and you perish from the way, when His Wrath is kindled but a little. Blessed are all they who put their trust in Him"* (Ps. 2:11-12).

Today we have a choice to serve God or not to serve God. But in that day men will be obliged to accept and obey God's Laws or else be smitten and punished on the spot! Millions of people from all over the world will hear the Word of God and will obey the Laws of the King of kings. Lawbreaking immediately will be stopped, and justice and righteousness will prevail.

The King's Rule will be universal (Zech. 14:9). The Angel Gabriel, in the Annunciation, told the Virgin Mary to name the Holy Child, Jesus, for . . .

"He shall be great, and shall be called the Son of the Highest: and the Lord God shall give unto Him the Throne of His father David:
"And He shall reign . . . and OF HIS KINGDOM THERE SHALL BE NO END" (Lk. 1:32-33).

Isaiah had prophesied centuries before Christ's First Advent:

"And THE GOVERNMENT SHALL BE UPON HIS SHOULDER: and His Name shall be called Wonderful, Counselor, The Mighty God, The Everlasting Father, The Prince of Peace.
"OF THE INCREASE OF HIS GOVERNMENT AND PEACE THERE SHALL BE NO END, upon the Throne of David, and upon His Kingdom, to order it, and to establish it with judgment and with justice from henceforth even forever. The zeal of the LORD of Hosts will perform this" (Isa. 9:6-7).

One other beautiful piece of Prophecy speaks, first, of the fact of Jesus' Kingship and, second, of the character of His Reign.

> *"But unto the Son He said, Your Throne, O God, is forever and ever: a sceptre of Righteousness is the sceptre of Your Kingdom"* (Heb. 1:8).

A Righteous King ruling over a Righteous Kingdom — a Kingdom that stretches from east to west and from pole to pole. Glory to God! This is both the coming Kingdom and the coming King!

Jesus the King will also rule this Planet with a rod of iron.

> *"Why do the heathen rage, and the people imagine a vain thing? . . .*
> *"Yet have I set My King upon My Holy Hill of Zion.*
> *"I will declare the decree. . . .*
> *"Ask of Me, and I shall give You the heathen for Your inheritance, and the uttermost parts of the Earth for Your possession.*
> *"YOU SHALL BREAK THEM WITH A ROD OF IRON"* (Ps. 2:1-9).

> *"And out of His Mouth goes a sharp sword, that with it He should smite the nations: and HE SHALL RULE THEM WITH A ROD OF IRON. . . .*
> *"And He has on His vesture and on His Thigh a Name written, KING OF KINGS, AND LORD OF LORDS"* (Rev. 19:15-16).

Although this will be a universal reign of Righteousness, many persons will chafe under this *"Jesus stuff"* just as many persons are doing today. These will submit to the Lordship of Jesus Christ only because of the *"rod of iron"* and they will wait for the moment when such Kingdom Age will close.

There will be required universal worship of the King of kings and the Lord of lords.

> *"God also has highly exalted Him, and given Him a Name which is above every name:*
> *"That AT THE NAME OF JESUS EVERY KNEE SHOULD BOW, of things in Heaven, and things in Earth, and things under the Earth;*
> *"And that EVERY TONGUE SHOULD CONFESS THAT JESUS CHRIST IS LORD, to the Glory of God the Father"* (Phil. 2:9-11).

As a result of a great missionary program, thousands upon thousands of people will be brought into the Kingdom of God. Denominations, sects, and doctrinal differences will be a thing of the past. There will be one Lord and one Faith.

Just as the splendor of King Solomon's . . .

> *"fame was in all the nations round about"* (I Ki. 4:31)

. . . and just as the Queen of Sheba, overwhelmed by the magnitude of his kingdom, could say . . .

> *"I believed not the words, until I came, and my eyes had seen it: and, behold, the half was not told me: your wisdom and prosperity exceed the fame which I heard"* (I Ki. 10:7)

. . . so far will the Millennial Kingdom exceed King Solomon's that it will pale into insignificance!

Isaiah wrote of the Millennial Kingdom:

> *"It shall come, that I will gather all nations and tongues; and they shall come, and see My Glory"* (Isa. 66:18).

Glory to God! What a Kingdom and what a King!

From the time of the ancient Pharaohs of Egypt, the great Caesars of Rome, and even to President Roosevelt's *"New Deal"* and President Lyndon Baines Johnson's *"New Society,"* rulers have tried to leave a legacy for themselves to history. Every ruler has tried to achieve this great *"something new and wonderful for everyone"* society.

But it has never worked in the past, the present, nor will it ever work in the future — no, not even once in all of human history — until the Lord Jesus Christ comes to rule and reign.

CAPITAL OF THE KINGDOM

Jerusalem will be the center of worship and government. It will have been rebuilt and restored, having great and marvelous splendor (I Chron. 23:25; II Chron. 33:4-7; Ps. 48:8; Isa. 2:2-4; 11:11 through 12:6; Jer. 17:25; Ezek. 34:1-31; 43:7; Joel 3:17, 20; Mic. 4:7; Zech. 8:3-23; 14:1-21; Acts 15:1-18).

It has been said that geographically Jerusalem is the center of the Earth. Jerusalem is located just off the Mediterranean Sea, the name *"Mediterranean"* meaning *"the middle of the Earth."* Hebrew scholars indicate

"Jerusalem" originally meant *"foundation"* of an ancient god, and later came to mean *"foundation of peace"* or *"habitation of peace"* — the City of Peace.

During Abraham's day *"Jerusalem"* was known as *"Salem"* (see Genesis 14:18). The city is mentioned 807 times in Scripture. The city has undergone many sieges throughout its long history, yet it was the capital of Israel from the time of King David to the reign of King Nebuchadnezzar of Babylon. Jerusalem will become the capital of the Antichrist during the Great Tribulation, and it will be the capital of God's eternal Kingdom under King Jesus.

Jesus will return from Heaven (as promised in Acts 1:11), and His Feet will literally touch down on the Mount of Olives (Zech. 14:4).

> *"I will make the PLACE OF MY FEET GLORIOUS.*
> *". . . all they who despised you shall bow themselves down at the soles of your feet; and they shall call you, The city of the LORD, The ZION OF THE HOLY ONE OF ISRAEL"* (Isa. 60:13-14).

Jerusalem will become the headquarters of the King and the Kingdom. Jesus Himself called it . . .

> *"the city of the great King"* (Mat. 5:35).

Jerusalem is the Holy City, a glorious city, where once Jesus was rejected as King and Lord. But *someday* He will be hailed as King Jesus.

> *"Great is the LORD, and greatly to be praised in the city of our God, in the mountain of His Holiness.*
> *"Beautiful for situation, THE JOY OF THE WHOLE EARTH, IS MOUNT ZION, on the sides of the north, THE CITY OF THE GREAT KING"* (Ps. 48:1-2).

> *"Lift up your heads, O ye gates; and be ye lift up, ye everlasting doors; and the KING OF GLORY SHALL COME IN.*
> *"Who is this King of Glory? The LORD strong and mighty, the LORD mighty in battle.*
> *"Lift up your heads, O ye gates; even lift them up, ye everlasting doors; and the King of Glory shall come in.*
> *"Who is this King of Glory? The LORD of Hosts, HE IS THE KING OF GLORY"* (Ps. 24:7-10).

> *"His Eyes were as a flame of fire, and on His Head were*

many crowns; and He had a Name written, that no man knew, but He Himself.

"And He has on His vesture and on His Thigh a name written, KING OF KINGS, AND LORD OF LORDS" (Rev. 19:12, 16).

Throngs of worshipers will come daily to the world capital, Jerusalem, to worship King Jesus.

"And it shall come to pass, that from one new moon to another, and from one Sabbath to another, shall all flesh come to worship before Me, saith the LORD" (Isa. 66:23).

TEMPLE

There will be a Millennial Temple for the Jews. This Temple, with its enclosure called *"the sanctuary,"* will be one mile square (Ezek. 45:1-4). This will not be the Temple built in the days before the Second Coming of Christ, where the Antichrist will rule for the last half of the Great Tribulation (Mat. 24:15-22; II Thess. 2:4). That Temple will be destroyed when Christ returns. This Millennial Temple will be built by Christ Himself when He comes back to Earth to set up His earthly Kingdom. It will be Christ's earthly Throne forever (Ezek. 43:7).

"Behold the Man Whose Name is The BRANCH; and He shall grow up out of His place, and He shall build THE TEMPLE OF THE LORD:

"Even He shall build THE TEMPLE OF THE LORD; and He shall bear the Glory, and shall sit and rule upon His Throne; and He shall be a Priest upon His Throne: and the counsel of peace shall be . . . in THE TEMPLE OF THE LORD" (Zech. 6:12-14).

There will be Priests in this Temple as there were in the first Temple. Descendants of Levi will be involved in service, and the sons of Zadok who have been true to the house of David will do some of the most holy work (II Sam. 8:17; 15:24; 20:25; I Ki. 1:39; Ezek. 43:19-27; 44:9-31). It is indicated that the priesthood of Moses and of his Law is an *eternal* one (Ex. 29:9; 40:15; Num. 25:11-13; I Chron. 23:13).

"The holy portion of the land shall be for the PRIESTS THE MINISTERS OF THE SANCTUARY, which shall come near to minister unto the LORD: and it shall be a place for

their houses, and an Holy Place for the Sanctuary" (Ezek. 45:4).

This, however, is not in conflict with Hebrews 7:11-28, for there will be a change in the approach to Salvation and mediation with God, although the basic requirements will exist. Christ is our Passover, sacrificed once and forever, as contrasted to the regular offerings and sacrifices. The offerings of the priesthood will be not for Salvation, but for a memorial and object lesson to show the people what *already* has been accomplished through Christ. These offerings will be as Communion is today: a memorial regarding what Jesus did in His redemptive Work at Calvary.

In Ezekiel, Chapters 43 through 46 nearly all of the feasts that were observed by the Jews are mentioned as being celebrated in the Millennial Kingdom. These offerings and feasts, new moons and Sabbaths, and various ordinances and activities will be observed during the Millennium and in the New Earth forever (Isa. 66:22-24; Ezek. 44:5; 45:17; 46:1-3).

It will be a massive Temple, far beyond anything that the Earth has ever known. The Shekinah, the Glory of the Lord, will be there continually, for it is the Shekinah that makes this massive building a Holy Temple.

"And I will shake all nations, and the desire of all nations shall come, and I WILL FILL THIS HOUSE WITH GLORY, saith the LORD of Hosts.

"The silver is Mine, and the gold is Mine, saith the LORD of Hosts.

"THE GLORY OF THIS LATTER HOUSE SHALL BE GREATER THAN OF THE FORMER, saith the LORD of Hosts: and in this place will I give peace, saith the LORD of Hosts" (Hag. 2:7-9).

King Jesus also will be there.

"Behold the Man Whose name is THE BRANCH . . . He shall build the Temple of the LORD" (Zech. 6:12).

The Patriarch Abraham . . .

"looked for a city . . . Whose Builder and Maker is God" (Heb. 11:10).

One translation reads: *"whose Architect and Builder is God."* So it will be with the Millennial Temple: its *"Builder and Maker"* will be the

Lord of Glory!

Flowing out from the Millennial Temple will be a literal river. It will flow eastward and from the south side of the Altar, and then will turn to go southward through Jerusalem, dividing the city, with half of the river flowing westward into the Mediterranean Sea and the other half flowing into the Dead Sea. The Dead Sea will be healed, so that once again life will exist in it, with multitudes of fish and sea life (Ezek. 47:1-12; Zech. 14:8).

> *"Afterward He brought me again unto the door of the house; and, behold, WATERS ISSUED OUT from under the threshold of the house eastward . . . and IT WAS A RIVER that I could not pass over: for the waters were risen, waters to swim in, A RIVER THAT COULD NOT BE PASSED OVER"* (Ezek. 47:1-5).

A great earthquake will take place at the Second Coming of Christ when He sets His Foot on the Mount of Olives, causing a significant change for the whole country (Zech. 14:4-5). The Dead Sea will be provided an outlet to purify its stagnant waters, having been raised so that it can give life and sustenance.

> *"His Feet shall stand in that day upon the Mount of Olives, which is before Jerusalem on the east, and THE MOUNT OF OLIVES SHALL CLEAVE IN THE MIDST THEREOF toward the east and toward the west, and there shall be a very great valley; and HALF OF THE MOUNTAIN SHALL REMOVE TOWARD THE NORTH, AND HALF OF IT TOWARD THE SOUTH.*
>
> *"And you shall flee . . . like as you fled from before the EARTHQUAKE in the days of Uzziah king of Judah: and the LORD my God shall come, and all the Saints with you"* (Zech. 14:4-5).

KNOWLEDGE OF THE LORD

The Holy Spirit will be outpoured as never before during the Millennial Reign (Joel 2:28-29). God's Promise of a universal, worldwide spiritual awakening — even with the Salvation of millions of persons today and the infilling of the Holy Spirit — has not been *fully* fulfilled and will not be *fully* fulfilled until the Millennium.

During the Millennium multiplied hundreds of millions people will be Saved by the Blood of Jesus Christ — just as is happening today.

Then millions of people will be baptized in the Holy Spirit as recorded by the Prophet Joel (Joel 2:28-29).

In other words, what was received by the Early Church is being received today and will be received to a greater extent throughout the ages from the time the Messiah comes to bring universal peace and prosperity to all.

There will be universal knowledge of the Lord.

"For the Earth shall be FULL of the KNOWLEDGE OF THE LORD, as the waters cover the sea" (Isa. 11:9).

"For the Earth shall be FILLED with the KNOWLEDGE OF THE GLORY OF THE LORD, as the waters cover the sea" (Hab. 2:14).

This means that all people will know of the Ways of the Lord. There will not be people ignorant of His Ways as they are today. There will not be Gentile missionaries pleading that *"some have never heard."* For all will have heard — from the least to the greatest.

In that day there will be Jewish missionaries. That may sound strange, but nevertheless true. The Jewish people will become Messianic missionaries, preaching the Gospel of the Lord Jesus Christ. Of course, the glorified redeemed of the Lord will assist them, but basically it will be the Jews who will serve as missionaries because they will be the *"natural"* people (not glorified) in a natural setting.

"In those days it shall come to pass, that ten men shall take hold out of all languages of the nations, even shall take hold of the skirt of him who is a Jew, saying, We will go with you: for we have heard that God is with you" (Zech. 8:23).

The Promise was given to Abraham that his seed would be a Blessing to all nations. And one way in which they will bless the world is that they will carry out a missionary program such as we have today.

"How beautiful upon the mountains are the Feet of Him Who brings good tidings, Who publishes peace; Who brings good tidings of good, Who publishes Salvation; Who says unto Zion, Your God reigns!

"Your watchmen shall lift up the voice; with the voice together shall they sing: for they shall see eye to eye, when the LORD shall bring again Zion.

"Break forth into joy, sing together, you waste places of

Jerusalem: for the LORD has comforted His People, He has redeemed Jerusalem.

"The LORD has made bare His Holy Arm in the eyes of all the nations; and ALL THE ENDS OF THE EARTH SHALL SEE THE SALVATION OF OUR GOD" (Isa. 52:7-10).

During the Millennium there will be conversion experiences — just as today. In addition, there will be experiences of Divine healing — just as today.

"Strengthen ye the weak hands, and confirm the feeble knees.

"Say to them who are of a fearful heart, Be strong, fear not: behold, your God will come with vengeance, even God with a recompence; He will come and save you.

"THEN THE EYES OF THE BLIND SHALL BE OPENED, AND THE EARS OF THE DEAF SHALL BE UNSTOPPED.

"THEN SHALL THE LAME MAN LEAP AS AN HART, AND THE TONGUE OF THE DUMB SING: for in the wilderness shall waters break out, and streams in the desert" (Isa. 35:3-6).

During the Millennium it will be popular to serve God. There will not be many religions and many faiths, and many ways to find God. There will be one Faith, and it will be the Salvation of the Lord Jesus Christ.

"And it shall come to pass in the last days, that the mountain of the LORD's house shall be established in the top of the mountains, and shall be exalted above the hills; and all nations shall flow unto it.

"And many people shall go and say, Come ye, and let us go up to the mountain of the LORD, to the House of the God of Jacob; and He will teach us of His Ways, and we will walk in His Paths: for out of Zion shall go forth the Law, and the Word of the LORD from Jerusalem" (Isa. 2:2-3).

PEACE ON EARTH

During the Millennium there will be universal peace. The Promise of the Angel to the shepherds will be a *full* reality.

"For unto you is born this day in the city of David a Saviour, which is Christ the Lord.

"And this shall be a sign unto you; You shall find the baby

wrapped in swaddling clothes, lying in a manger.
"Glory to God in the highest, AND ON EARTH PEACE,
GOOD WILL TOWARD MEN" (Lk. 2:11-12, 14).

This means there will be no taxation to keep up large armies and navies. The universal conversation will be not about war, treaties, armament, depression, varied religions, and forms of government, but about the goodness and greatness of God and the wonder of His Reign. People will be fully satisfied in peace and prosperity (Isa. 2:4; 9:6-7; Mic. 4:3-4; Mal. 1:11).

"And He shall judge among the nations, and shall rebuke many people: and they shall beat their swords into plowshares, and their spears into pruninghooks: nation shall not lift up sword against nation, neither shall they learn war any more" (Isa. 2:4).

"And He shall judge among many people, and rebuke strong nations afar off; and they shall beat their swords into plowshares, and their spears into pruninghooks: nation shall not lift up a sword against nation, neither shall they learn war any more.
"But they shall sit every man under his vine and under his fig tree; and none shall make them afraid; for the Mouth of the LORD of Hosts has spoken it" (Mic. 4:3-4).

There will be no harboring of prejudice, racism, nationalism, bigotry, jealousy, or an undercurrent of unrest. Instead spiritual awakenings will take place in every land. And as people turn to God, they will be united in serving Christ. Attention will turn from recession, depression, war, the cold war, to *"tell me more about Jesus!"* People will live in an idyllic state of Peace and absence of tension, knowing the Goodness and Blessing of God.

"For from the rising of the sun even unto the going down of the same My Name shall be great among the Gentiles; and in every place incense shall be offered unto My Name, and a pure offering: for My Name shall be great among the heathen, saith the LORD of Hosts" (Mal. 1:11).

"For all people will walk every one in the name of his god, and we will walk in the Name of the LORD our God forever and ever" (Mic. 4:5).

During the Millennium there will be neither need nor want, as man feeds on universal prosperity (Isa. 65:24; Mic. 4:4-5). Unemployment and poverty will cease to exist because there will not be great amounts of money wasted on foolishness, entertainment, debauchery, lasciviousness, licentiousness, and carousing as in our present day.

Tithing was practiced *before* the Law (Gen. 14:20; 28:22), *under* the Law (Lev. 27:30-33), and *since* the Law (Mat. 23:23; I Cor. 9:7-18; 16:1-3). And tithing will be practiced in the Millennium. Tithing will supply ample provision for everyone. Since there will be no need for massive taxation to care for a national defense, a welfare state, or social ills, money will be free to promote the Gospel of the Kingdom.

During the Millennium this reign of Peace and Prosperity will extend to the animal kingdom, as well (Isa. 11:6-8; 65:17-25; Rom. 8:18-23). Their very nature will be transformed. No longer will they be fierce; they will not kill; they will not be poisonous.

"The wolf also shall dwell with the lamb, and the leopard shall lie down with the kid; and the calf and the young lion and the fatling together; and a little child shall lead them.

"And the cow and the bear shall feed; their young ones shall lie down together: and the lion shall eat straw like the ox.

"And the suckling child shall play on the hole of the asp, and the weaned child shall put his hand on the cockatrice' den.

"They shall not hurt nor destroy in all My holy mountain: for the Earth shall be full of the Knowledge of the LORD, as the waters cover the sea" (Isa. 11:6-9).

This means that the carnivorous nature of the wild beast will be gone. Even naturally ferocious beasts, like the lion, will become vegetarian, and *"shall eat straw like the ox."*

Not only will the beasts be at peace between themselves, but they will be at peace with man. The baby, the toddler, the little schoolchild will be safe from all harm even if he puts his hand into a nest of rattlesnakes!

Not only will the beasts be at peace with man, but man will be at peace with the beasts. There will be no more African safaris for the sake of big-time game hunting. There will be no more deer season, or hunting and fishing license. Why? Because the curse has been lifted, and the Knowledge of the Lord will cover the Earth as the waters cover the sea. Even natural disasters — tornadoes, earthquakes, volcanic eruptions, tidal waves, storms, floods, hurricanes, snowstorms, avalanches, rock slides, great cyclones, and twisters — will vanish from the Earth. There will be *rest* in the very elements themselves.

A TIME OF RESTORATION

During the Millennium the living conditions will be a dream fulfilled. The earth will produce abundantly, and no one will want for the necessities of life. People will live free of worry for material things. People will cease to fret because of their being subject to droughts, crop failure, lay-offs, strikes, crime, and widespread dishonesty — simply because these things will not exist in the Kingdom.

The Earth will cease to groan and travail, as it does now (Rom. 8:22), for the time of deliverance will have come, and it will be the birth of a New Age.

"Who has heard such a thing?. . . for as soon as Zion travailed, she brought forth her children.

"Shall I bring to the birth, and not cause to bring forth?. . .

"Rejoice ye with Jerusalem, and be glad with her, all ye who love her. . . .

"That you may suck, and be satisfied with the breasts of her consolations; that you may milk out, and be delighted with the ABUNDANCE OF HER GLORY.

"For thus saith the LORD, Behold, I will extend PEACE TO HER LIKE A RIVER, and the glory of the Gentiles LIKE A FLOWING STREAM: then shall you suck, you shall be borne upon her sides, and be dandled upon her knees.

"AS ONE WHOM HIS MOTHER COMFORTS, SO WILL I COMFORT YOU; and you shall be comforted in Jerusalem.

"And when you see this, YOUR HEART SHALL REJOICE, AND YOUR BONES SHALL FLOURISH LIKE AN HERB" (Isa. 66:8-14).

The Earth will be restored to the wonderful beauty and abundance of its original creation (Isa. 35:1-10; 55:12-13; Ezek. 36:8-12; Joel 2:18-27; 3:17-21; Amos 9:13-15; Rom. 8:18-23; II Pet., Chpt. 3). All lands will be restored to a wonderful fruitfulness (with the exception of those few lands that will remain under an abiding curse, such as Babylon). The ugliness and blight that characterizes so much of the world today because of sin and rebellion against God will be erased and a great restoration will take place (read Jer., Chpts. 50 and 51).

"The wilderness and the solitary place shall be glad for them; and the desert shall rejoice, and blossom as the rose.

"It shall blossom ABUNDANTLY, and rejoice even with

joy and singing. . . .

"And the parched ground shall become a pool, and the thirsty land springs of water: in the habitation of dragons, where each lay, shall be grass with reeds and rushes.

"And AN HIGHWAY SHALL BE THERE, AND A WAY, and it shall be called The Way of Holiness; the unclean shall not pass over it; but it shall be for those: the wayfaring men, though fools, shall not err therein.

"No lion shall be there, nor any ravenous beast shall go up thereon, it shall not be found there; but the redeemed shall walk there:

"And the ransomed of the LORD shall return, and come to Zion with songs and EVERLASTING JOY upon their heads: they shall obtain joy and gladness, and sorrow and sighing shall flee away" (Isa. 35:1-2, 7-10).

Love and Righteousness will prevail. There will be an increase of light. The Land of Promise will become the Land of Plenty, just as rich and succulent as in the days of Joshua and Caleb . . .

"a land which flows with milk and honey" (Num. 14:8; cf. 13:17 through 14:8).

"Then shall He give the rain of your seed, that you shall sow the ground withal; and bread of the increase of the Earth, and it shall be fat and plenteous: in that day shall your cattle feed in large pastures.

"The oxen likewise and the young asses that ear the ground shall eat clean provender, which has been winnowed with the shovel and with the fan.

"Moreover the light of the moon shall be as the light of the sun, and the light of the sun shall be sevenfold, as the light of seven days, in the day that the LORD binds up the breach of His People, and heals the stroke of their wound" (Isa. 30:23-24, 26).

"Whereas you have been forsaken and hated, so that no man went through you, I will make you an eternal excellency, a joy of many generations.

"You shall also suck the milk of the Gentiles, and shall suck the breast of kings: and you shall know that I the LORD am your Saviour and your Redeemer, The Mighty One of Jacob.

"For brass I will bring gold, and for iron I will bring silver, and for wood brass, and for stones iron: I will also make your

officers peace, and your exactors righteousness.

"Violence shall no more be heard in your land, wasting nor destruction within your borders; but you shall call your walls Salvation, and your gates Praise.

"The sun shall be no more your light by day; neither for brightness shall the moon give light unto you: but the LORD shall be unto you an everlasting Light, and your God your Glory.

"Your people also shall be all righteous: they shall inherit the land forever" (Isa. 60:15-19, 21).

During the Millennium human life will be prolonged. The longevity of the Patriarchal Era will be experienced again. Men will live to 1,000 years, and then those who do not rebel against God, with Satan, at the end of the Millennium, will live on and on without seeing death (Isa. 65:20; Zech. 8:4).

Man was created to live a long time: Adam lived 900 years; Methuselah lived to be 969 years old; and Enoch lived 365 years on Earth. The human body actually renews itself every seven years, and without the curse it will be able to live on indefinitely.

"There shall be no more thence an infant of days, nor an old man who has not filled his days: for the child shall die an hundred years old; but the sinner being an hundred years old shall be accursed.

"And they shall build houses, and inhabit them; and they shall plant vineyards, and eat the fruit of them.

"They shall not build, and another inhabit; they shall not plant, and another eat: for as the days of a tree are the days of My People, and My Elect shall long enjoy the work of their hands" (Isa. 65:20-22).

Today if a man plants a tree, he may not live to see it grow to a swelling size. If he builds a house, a business, an empire, he may not live to enjoy its harvest. Too many times a man's heirs are the recipients of the blessings he labored so hard to earn. But this observation will not be true in that day, for men will live to enjoy the fruit of their own labors.

PURPOSE OF GOD

The entire Program of God in this Kingdom Age will have behind it a number of Divine Purposes:

1. TO BEGIN THE RESTITUTION OF ALL THINGS THAT

ADAM LOST IN THE GARDEN OF EDEN AND TO FUL-FILL HIS DIVINE PLAN FOR MAN (Acts 3:21; I Cor. 15:24-28; Eph. 1:10);

2. TO JUDGE THE NATIONS IN RIGHTEOUSNESS AND TO RESTORE THE EARTH TO ITS RIGHTFUL OWNERS (Isa. 2:2-4; 11:1-11; Mat. 25:31-46);

3. TO PUT UNDER HIS FEET ALL ENEMIES AND ALL RE-BELLION AS MAN'S FINAL TEST COMES TO A CLOSE (I Cor. 15:24-28; Heb. 2:7-9; Eph. 1:10);

4. TO RESTORE THE NATION OF ISRAEL AND TO DELIVER HER FROM OTHER NATIONS AND TO MAKE ISRAEL THE HEAD AND NOT THE TAIL (Deut. 28:13; Isa. 11:1; Ezek. 20:33-44; Acts 15:13-17);

5. TO FULFILL THE EVERLASTING COVENANTS MADE WITH ABRAHAM (Gen., Chpts. 12; 26; 28; 35) AND WITH DAVID (II Sam., Chpt. 7);

6. TO VINDICATE AND AVENGE CHRIST AND HIS SAINTS (Mat. 26:63-66; Rom. 12:19; I Pet. 1:10-11);

7. TO EXALT THE SAINTS OF ALL AGES TO SERVE AS KINGS AND PRIESTS BEFORE GOD AND TO REWARD THEM ACCORDING TO GOD'S PROMISE (Rom. 8:17-21; 14:10-11; I Cor., Chpt. 6; II Cor. 5:10; Phil. 3:20-21; Col. 3:4; I Pet. 1:10-13; 5:1, 4; Rev. 1:5; 2:26; 5:10; 11:18; 12:5; 20:4-6); AND,

8. TO ESTABLISH A RIGHTEOUS AND ETERNAL GOV-ERNMENT ON EARTH (Isa. 9:6-7; 11:1-9; 42:1-5; Dan. 2:44-45; 7:13-27; Lk. 1:32-35; Rev. 11:15; 19:11-16; 20:4-6; 22:5).

The Millennial Reign will be the greatest age the world has ever known. Jesus Christ personally will reign supreme from Jerusalem. King David will reign over all of Israel under the Lord Jesus Christ. Every Saint who has ever lived from the time of Adam to the Millennium will be here in his glorified body. Then the world will know what it could have had all of these millennia that it lived in rebellion against God. Then it will know the peace and prosperity that God intended from the beginning of time.

FINAL CONFLICT

Much has been written concerning the Battle of Armageddon as the battle to end all battles and usher in the Millennium. However, little has been written about the last and final conflict of the ages, and that is the battle that issues in eternity — the Battle of Gog and Magog.

The final battle will see the failure of Satan's last attempt at rebellion, resulting in his being cast into eternal fire, the renovation of Planet Earth, the final Judgment of all unrighteousness, and the beginning of eternity.

It seems that Satan being loosed for a season indicates more of the nature of God than of the wickedness of Satan. God will allow Satan liberty, take it from him, and give it to him again — not because Satan is useful to Him, but to show His Power to bring good out of evil, to make His enemies praise Him, and to turn the Devil's wickedness to further the very Purpose that Satan desired to defeat.

Yet after being bound for 1,000 years, Satan's diabolical plan will not have changed nor will he have reformed. Like Judas Iscariot, Satan will be given a final opportunity to make a better record for himself. But neither Mercy nor Judgment will have any effect on him.

> *"And when the thousand years are expired, Satan shall be loosed out of his prison,*
>
> *"And shall go out to deceive the nations which are in the four quarters of the Earth, GOG AND MAGOG, to gather them together to BATTLE: the number of whom is as the sand of the sea.*
>
> *"And they went up on the breadth of the Earth, and compassed the camp of the Saints about, and the beloved city: and fire came down from God out of Heaven, and devoured them.*
>
> *"And the Devil who deceived them was cast into the Lake of Fire and brimstone, where the Beast and the False Prophet are, and shall be tormented day and night forever and ever"* (Rev. 20:7-10).

The term *"Gog and Magog"* is somewhat confusing to Bible scholars as the term is used also in Ezekiel, Chapters 38 and 39, there with a pre-Millennial reference. Here *"Gog and Magog"* refers to the rebelling Gentiles as indicated from Satan deceiving the nations . . .

> *"which are in the four quarters of the Earth."*

Satan's appeal will be to those nations that dwell in the farthest reaches of the Earth. As we have already mentioned, thousands of people on Earth during the Millennium will be unimpressed by the Rule of the Lord Jesus Christ and will wait for the right opportunity and the right man to come along and overthrow this new Kingdom.

In the past Satan's strongest influence and activity has been among the less-civilized nations of the world. This may be the same scenario that is portrayed here in Revelation, Chapter 20. How Satan accomplishes this rebellion we are not told. But at his bidding hordes will come swarming into the Holy Land and encompass the Holy City in a vain hope of taking it from King Jesus. What folly!

It is almost unbelievable that hordes of people . . .

"the number of whom is as the sand of the sea"

. . . would once again, after 1,000 years of Peace and Righteousness, attempt another Armageddon, yet they will! But is it any wonder when we consider that those for whom Jesus came to reign and establish a Kingdom for which they had longed for, for thousands of years, would reject and crucify Him?

Or consider that in our own day millions of Westerners still choose Satan in spite of all the Gospel that is being preached worldwide.

Yet Jesus allows it.

In that day teeming millions of persons will go to Hell in a last-ditch effort to overthrow the Lord Jesus Christ. Millions of persons will be absolute fools — what insanity to rebel against Peace and Righteousness!

It is here that we are given insight into the true meaning of the word *"zapped."* For Scripture tells us that the battle will be over far more quickly than it began. In a moment of time the evil one and his millions of ignorant followers will be *"zapped."*

"They went up . . . and FIRE CAME DOWN FROM GOD OUT OF HEAVEN, AND DEVOURED THEM."

What a tragic waste! Yet what Power and Judgment belongs to the Lion of the Tribe of Judah who . . .

"has prevailed" (Rev. 5:5).

So ends the final conflict.

FINAL JUDGMENT

After the Battle of Gog and Magog will come what scholars call the Great White Throne Judgment.

"And I saw a GREAT WHITE THRONE, and Him Who sat on it, from Whose face the Earth and the Heaven fled away;

and there was found no place for them.

"And I saw the dead, small and great, stand before God; and THE BOOKS WERE OPENED: and another Book was opened, which is the Book of Life: and THE DEAD WERE JUDGED OUT OF THOSE THINGS WHICH WERE WRITTEN IN THE BOOKS, according to their works.

"And the sea gave up the dead which were in it; and Death and Hell delivered up the dead which were in them: and they were judged every man according to their works.

"And Death and Hell were cast into the Lake of Fire. This is the second death. And whosoever was not found written in the Book of Life was cast into the Lake of Fire" (Rev. 20:11-15).

This Judgment will come after the Millennium and the Battle of Gog and Magog.

It is stated in this Passage that Heaven and Earth will flee from before His *"Face."* The Greek word for *"face"* is *prosopon,* meaning *"countenance, aspect, appearance, surface, front view, outward appearance, face, even person."* It indicates that God has an outward Appearance and a real Body. The word is used nine times in the Book of Revelation (4:7; 6:16; 7:11; 9:7; 10:1; 11:16; 12:14; 20:11; 22:4). In other places in the New Testament this same word has reference to a bodily presence and its actual appearance.

Many things may be observed concerning the Great White Throne Judgment:

1. GOD IS THE JUDGE, AND YET GOD THE SON IS ALSO SPOKEN OF AS JUDGE (Jn. 5:19-27; Acts 10:42; 17:30-31; II Tim. 4:8; Rev. 19:11).

2. ALL THE WICKED DEAD FROM ADAM TO THE TIME OF JUDGMENT WILL BE JUDGED (Acts 17:31; Rom. 3:6; Rev. 20:11-15). However, this will not include the Beast, the False Prophet, the goat nations, or the tares (Mat. 13:24-30; 25:31-46; Rev. 19:20). Those judged at the Judgment of the Nations will not be in this Great White Throne Judgment. Sentence will have been pronounced on them 1,000 years earlier, and that Judgment need not be repeated.

3. THIS JUDGMENT WILL TAKE PLACE AFTER THE MILLENNIUM AND AFTER SATAN HAS BEEN CAST INTO THE LAKE OF FIRE (Rev. 20:7-11).

4. IT IS SPECIFIED AS A *"DAY"* OF JUDGMENT (Mat. 10:15;

11:22, 24; 12:36; Mk. 6:11; II Pet. 2:9; 3:7; I Jn. 4:17; Jude, Vs. 6). It is set at a definite time.

5. IT TAKES PLACE BEFORE THE THRONE OF GOD (Rev. 20:11). At this time the Throne is still in Heaven. A similar Throne was seen by John the Revelator at the beginning of the great Judgment, which preceded the Millennium (Rev. 4:2-6). That Judgment was set in Heaven. Also, that Judgment has a rainbow over it, to indicate the fulfillment of Covenant Promises. This Great White Throne Judgment has nothing over it, for it has no hope to offer to anyone, no covenant of good to fulfill. (Refer to Rev. 4:2-3.)

6. THIS JUDGMENT IS DESCRIBED AS *"GREAT"* AND *"WHITE"* (Rev. 20:11-12), indicative of immeasurable power and complete justice. There will be no more probation and no more threat of coming Judgment. The first mention of God's Throne, had around it 24 Elders, taking part in administration. Also, there were . . .

"seven lamps of fire burning before the Throne, which are the Seven Spirits of God" (Rev. 4:4-5)

. . . indicating Grace and Mercy. By contrast, the Great White Throne Judgment is unaccompanied by Grace and Mercy.

7. THIS JUDGMENT IS CHARACTERIZED BY HOPELESS- NESS AND DOOM. The first mention of the Throne of God pictures the 24 Elders with harps, singing a new song, worshipping with a loud voice, giving praise to the King of kings — the Lamb that sits upon the Throne (Rev., Chpt. 5). At the Great White Throne Judgment there is no song, no gladness, no exaltation, be- cause it is the sentencing of the wicked to their eternal punishment.

8. AT THIS TIME ALL THE SECRETS OF MEN — EVERY IDLE WORD, THEIR WORKS, THEIR THOUGHTS, THEIR DEEDS — WILL BE BROUGHT INTO JUDGMENT (Rom. 2:16; Mat. 12:36). God will not condemn or punish one indi- vidual until he stands trial and understands clearly the reason for his punishment. God is a Just God (Rev. 15:3). No excuse will stand long before His all-searching Eye, His all-knowing Record.

"Every mouth may be stopped, and all the world may be- come guilty before God . . . there shall no flesh be justified in

His sight" (Rom. 3:19-20).

"As I live, saith the Lord, every knee shall bow to Me, and every tongue shall confess to God.

"So then every one of us shall give account of himself to God" (Rom. 14:11-12).

The Book of Life will be opened and every man's works will be revealed.

9. THE DEAD WILL NOT INCLUDE ANGELS, BUT MOR-TALS WHO HAVE DIED AND GONE TO HELL. As we know, Hell is a different place from the Lake of Fire or *"eternal Hell,"* because . . .

"Death and Hell were cast into the Lake of Fire."

Hades is the present place of confinement for the souls of the wicked, and there they are conscious and in torment until the Resurrection.

10. THE DEAD WILL BE JUDGED OUT OF THE BOOK OF LIFE. This Book will have in it the names of those who have entered into life and who are committed to the Lord. Basically, the reference to Books in Revelation 20:12 relates to the Word of God, which will judge men.

HELL

"Hell" is the word generally used to translate the Hebrew *sheol*.

1. HELL IS DEEP AND DARK (Job 11:8; Chpts. 21-22);

2. HELL IS IN THE HEART OF THE EARTH (Num. 16:30; Deut. 32:22);

3. HELL IS FASTENED WITH GATES AND BARS (Job 17:16; 38:17; Isa. 38:10);

4. HELL IS THE HABITATION OF DEAD MEN AND EVIL SPIRITS (Ps. 86:13; 89:48; Prov. 13:14; Ezek. 31:17; 32:21); AND,

5. HELL IS A PLACE OF TORMENT (Lk. 16:23; II Pet. 2:4; Mat. 11:23).

LAKE OF FIRE

The Lake of Fire, by contrast, is not the place where dead men are *now* awaiting Judgment. Whereas *"Hell"* is the *intermediate* place of punishment between death and the resurrection of the unrighteous dead, the *"Lake of Fire"* will be the *eternal* place of punishment. The most frequent word used to describe this place is the Greek *gehenna*.

The place of eternal damnation will have degrees of punishment and torment and fire, just as Heaven will have degrees of reward and bliss and comfort for those pronounced . . .

"good and faithful" (Mat. 25:14-30).

The degrees of punishment may mean degrees of mental torment, as men agonize over the awareness of their evil deeds and the realization that they refused to commit their life to Christ.

Punishment will be eternal. Those who receive Life have the Promise of God that they will have . . .

"Everlasting Life" (Jn. 3:16).

The same Greek word *aionion*, meaning *"forever," "without end,"* is used of eternal damnation (Mat. 25:41, 46; Heb. 6:2; 10:26-31; Rev. 14:9-11; 19:20; 20:10-15; 21:8).

The Lake of Fire is a place characterized by . . .

1. OUTER DARKNESS (Mat. 8:12; 22:13; 25:30);

2. WEEPING (Mat. 8:12; 22:13; 24:51; 25:30; Lk. 13:28);

3. WAILING (Mat. 13:42, 50);

4. GNASHING OF TEETH (Mat. 8:12; 13:42, 50; 22:13; 24:51; 25:30);

5. FIRE (Mat. 7:19; 13:40-50; 18:8; 25:41; Mk. 9:43-49);

6. BRIMSTONE (Rev. 19:20; 20:10; 21:8);

7. CARNALITY (Mk. 9:43-49);

8. TORMENT (Lk. 16:28; Rev. 14:9-12);

9. SMOKE (Rev. 14:11); AND,

10. REMORSE (Lk. 16:19-31).

Chapter 6

The New Heaven And New Earth

CHAPTER SIX

THE NEW HEAVEN AND NEW EARTH

We have now reached the end of the age and the dawn of eternity. The Millennium has ended. Satan has been judged and sentenced and cast into the Lake of Fire. The wicked dead have been raised, judged, and cast into the Lake of Fire. Now only eternity remains.

Everything will become new. Three times in Revelation, Chapter 21 the word *"new"* is used. And one of these three times it is used inclusively . . .

> *"Behold, I make ALL THINGS NEW"* (Rev. 21:5).

This does not mean that the present Earth will cease to exist, but that it will be *changed*. The teaching of Scripture is that the Creation is presently bound, in a state of captivity, tied down. The dissolving of these bonds (II Pet. 3:10-13) will not mean the destruction or annihilation of Planet Earth, but its liberation from the forces of evil and from the curses that have it bound.

The Promise is that . . .

> *"the meek . . . shall inherit the Earth"* (Mat. 5:5).

> *"those who wait upon the LORD . . . shall inherit the Earth.*
> *"the meek shall inherit the Earth. . . .*
> *"The righteous shall inherit the land, and DWELL THEREIN FOR EVER"* (Ps. 37:9, 11, 29).

> *"Your people . . . shall inherit the land forever"* (Isa. 60:21).

It stands to reason that if the righteous are to inherit the land forever, then it must exist forever. God covenanted with Abraham that a certain portion of the Earth (the Promised Land) would be . . .

> *"an everlasting possession"* (Gen. 17:8; cf. 15:18-21).

> *"And they shall dwell in the land that I have given unto Jacob My Servant, wherein your fathers have dwelt; and they shall dwell therein, even THEY, AND THEIR CHILDREN, AND THEIR CHILDREN'S CHILDREN FOREVER"* (Ezek. 37:25).

It would not be possible for these Promises to be fulfilled if the Earth were annihilated.

In Revelation 21:1 the word *"new"* is the Greek *kainos* and means *"new"* or *"renewed."* It carries the idea of freshness and character, and does not mean *"new"* in existence.

A contrast is found in Matthew 9:17 where the Word speaks of new wine (*neos, "newly made wine"*) being put into new bottles (*kainos, "freshened or renewed wine skins"*).

We conclude, then, that the expressions, *"New Heaven"* and *"New Earth"* (II Pet. 3:13; Rev. 21:1), have reference to the present Heaven and Earth being renewed in character; that is, loosed from the old curse with its corresponding influence and effect.

This New Earth will be one . . .

> *"wherein dwells Righteousness"* (II Pet. 3:13).

Whereas our present Earth is marked by the curse that fell after the Fall (Gen., Chpt. 3), the New Earth will be marked by the Blessing that comes from God — a divine benediction.

This will be the great climax to the eternal Plan of God. Since the beginning God has determined to dwell with His Creation in a perfect environment, free from sin, sickness, sorrow, and pain! He has longed to walk with man . . .

> *"in the cool of the day"* (Gen. 3:8)

. . . as He did in the Garden of Eden and to have eternal fellowship with him.

This will become a wonderful reality in the New Earth! With the extinction of the curse of sin and sin's effect upon Creation, man will truly enjoy *"Heaven on Earth!"*

NEW JERUSALEM

The Apostle John saw . . .

> *"the Holy City, New Jerusalem, coming down from God out of Heaven, prepared as a Bride adorned for her husband"* (Rev. 21:2)

. . . and he heard a voice saying . . .

"Behold, the Tabernacle of God is with men, and He will dwell with them, and they shall be His People, and God Himself shall be with them, and be their God" (Rev. 21:3).

God will dwell with, or tabernacle with, men (Jn. 1:14; Rev. 7:15; 12:12; 13:6). He will be visible to men and will be literally . . .

"Emmanuel . . . God with us" (Mat. 1:23; cf. Ps. 68:16-18; Isa. 7:14; Zech. 2:10-11; 8:3; Rev. 22:5).

God will wipe away all tears (Rev. 21:4; Isa. 25:8). *"To wipe"* is *"to stroke, rub, erase, touch, abolish, and utterly wipe away."* The things that cause sorrow and regret will be removed. The hands of man, the powers of Earth cannot go far in binding up broken hearts. It is only the Hands that were nailed to the Cross that can reach into the deepest resources of man's spirit and dry up the fountains of hurt and pain. Every tear — tears of grief, tears of misfortune, tears of poverty, tears of bereavement, tears of sympathy, tears of mercy, tears of persecution, tears of contrition, tears of penitence for faults and failures, tears of disappointment, tears of bitterness, tears of sickness — will be wiped away by the loving Hand of our God.

God will make an end not only of tears, but even of Death itself.

"There shall be no more death, neither sorrow, nor crying, neither shall there be any more pain: for the former things are passed away" (Rev. 21:4).

Everywhere we turn there is evidence of death and dying. We see graveyards filled with tombstones. We see memorials erected *"in memory of."* We see funeral processions and obituaries. Death is all around us. Foundations have been set up, and millions of dollars allocated to research, for the purpose of eliminating disease and early death. Still there is no remedy. Man must die.

However, the time is coming when death itself shall die! Hallelujah! This end will come not by the power or ingenuity of some bright genius, but by the Power of Almighty God! Then will come the literal fulfillment of the Apostle Paul's exclamation:

"Death is swallowed up in victory, O death, where is your sting?" (I Cor. 15:54-55; Isa. 25:8).

There will never be another deathbed scene, another grave dug, another funeral, another obituary, another grieving wife or mother, for death will be no more.

"All things new" . . . God has created all things; and man, His highest creation, was to have dominion over all the Works of His Hands (Ps. 8), including the Heavenly bodies — the Universe. It figures, then, that man's dominion will reach to this area of God's Creation in the future restoration.

The Holy City, the New Jerusalem, will have foundations, walls, gates, and streets. It will have guards outside and inhabitants within.

"Abraham looked for A CITY which has foundations, whose Builder and Maker is God" (Heb. 11:10).

"God has prepared for them A CITY" (Heb. 11:16).

Jesus promised His Disciples:

"I go to prepare A PLACE for you.
"And if I go and prepare A PLACE for you, I will come again, and receive you unto Myself; that where I am, there you may be also" (Jn. 14:2-3).

The Apostle Paul reiterated:

"Here have we no continuing city, but we seek one to come" (Heb. 13:14).

It is obvious that in the New Jerusalem we have a true city, a real city, a God-built city, a substantial and eternal city that fulfills the prophetic announcements.

It is called . . . *"the Bride, the Lamb's Wife"* (Rev. 21:9).

This means it will be inhabited by the Blood-washed, Blood-bought Saints of God and the Redeemed of all the ages.

The location of the New Jerusalem will be Earth itself, for we read that the city came . . .

"DOWN FROM GOD OUT OF HEAVEN, prepared as a Bride adorned for her husband" (Rev. 21:2).

"And the nations of them which are Saved shall walk in the light of it: and the kings OF THE EARTH do bring their glory and honour into it. . . . And they shall bring the glory and

honour of the nations into it" (Rev. 21:24, 26).

The Glory of God will be reflected throughout the city and is likened to a jasper stone (Rev. 21:11). A beautiful light of radiant glory will be seen throughout the New Jerusalem. The Lamb of God will be the Light of the city.

> *"And I saw no Temple therein: for the Lord God Almighty and the Lamb are the Temple of it.*
> *"And the city had no need of the sun, neither of the moon, to shine in it: for the Glory of God did lighten it, and the Lamb is the Light thereof"* (Rev. 21:22-23).

Everything built by God is the very best and most splendid of its kind, so it is also with this fabulous city. Noah's ark staggers the imagination. The glory of King Solomon's temple and kingdom is beyond our comprehension. And still all of these will someday pale in the light of God's sublime crowning achievement, this most marvelous of all His glorious Works.

This great City will be so huge that if we could imagine a city stretching from Boston to Miami and from New York City to Denver, and towering 1,500 miles into the air, we could visualize the dimensions of that place that is being prepared as our eternal abode.

> *"And had a wall great and high, and had TWELVE GATES, and at the gates TWELVE ANGELS, and names written thereon . . .*
> *"And the wall of the city had TWELVE FOUNDATIONS . . .*
> *"And THE CITY LIES FOURSQUARE, AND THE LENGTH IS AS LARGE AS THE BREADTH: AND HE MEASURED THE CITY WITH THE REED, TWELVE THOUSAND FURLONGS. THE LENGTH AND THE BREADTH AND THE HEIGHT OF IT ARE EQUAL"* (Rev. 21:12-16).

This great city is also adorned with costly jewels and precious metals.

> *"And the building of the wall of it was of JASPER: and the city was PURE GOLD, like unto clear glass.*
> *"And the foundations of the wall of the city were garnished with all manner of PRECIOUS STONES. The first foundation was JASPER; the second, SAPPHIRE; the third,*

a CHALCEDONY; the fourth, an EMERALD;

"The fifth, SARDONYX; the sixth, SARDIUS; the seventh, CHRYSOLYTE; the eighth, BERYL; the ninth, a TOPAZ; the tenth, a CHRYSOPRASUS; the eleventh, a JACINTH; the twelfth, an AMETHYST.

"And the twelve gates were twelve PEARLS; every several gate was of one PEARL: and the street of the city was PURE GOLD, as it were TRANSPARENT GLASS" (Rev. 21:18-21).

The light of the city shining through these various colors in the foundation reflects a dazzling beauty in keeping with the Glory of God and the Beauty of His Holiness. Just the thought of this beautiful city makes a person yearn to be in it!

The light of the city will be greater than that of the sun, moon, and stars. The brilliance of the Glory of God, whose magnificent beauty defies description, will surpass even the sun, which will be increased sevenfold during the Millennium (Isa. 30:26). This city will have no need for the sun and moon, but the sun and moon will continue to shine for the sake of other parts of the Earth. The dazzling light from the Glory of God shining out from this transparent city of gold will be beyond our present descriptive ability. The nations will walk by the means of the light of that city.

The traffic of that city will be made up of kings of the Earth bringing their glory and honor into it. Their glory as kings will go to honor, dignify, and promote this marvelous city. Everything of greatness and glory that is possessed will be offered to the service and honor of that great city. Therefore, the gates of the city will never be closed.

The winged seraphim will fly about, crying:

"Holy, holy, holy, is the LORD of Hosts: the whole Earth is full of His Glory" (Isa. 6:3).

This is the . . .

"mountain of His Holiness" (Ps. 48:1)

. . . the City where His Glory dwells. Therefore, no common or unclean thing can ever enter it, nor . . .

"any thing that defiles, neither whatsoever works abomination, or makes a lie: but they which are written in the Lamb's Book of Life" (Rev. 21:27).

The Psalmist once spoke of a . . .

> *"river, the streams whereof shall make glad the City of God, the Holy Place of the Tabernacles of the Most High"* (Ps. 46:4).

This is that . . .

> *"pure river of Water of Life, clear as crystal, proceeding out of the Throne of God and of the Lamb"* (Rev. 22:1).

Heaven will not be a place of dust and drought. It will have its glad springs of water, an ever-flowing river, issuing directly from the Throne of God.

Never has an earthly city produced the kind of pure River of Life that this city will produce abundantly. No longer will its inhabitants have to drink from the polluted streams of this world, but they will drink eternally of Pure Waters clear as crystal.

Next we read of the marvelous Tree of Life.

> *"In the midst of the street of it, and on either side of the river, was there the Tree of Life, which bear twelve manner of fruits, and yielded her fruit every month: and the leaves of the tree were for the healing of the nations"* (Rev. 22:2).

Each month this Tree of Life will bear a different kind of fruit, which will be a source of enjoyment for the nations.

Someone may ask, *"Will we eat in Heaven?"*

Jesus mentioned several times that there will be eating and drinking in the Kingdom of God (Mat. 26:29; Lk. 22:30). He likened the whole provision of His Grace to a banquet, a feast, a supper (Mat. 22:1-14; Lk. 14:12-24). After His transformation, from death to immortality, Jesus ate with the Disciples (Lk., Chpt. 24; Jn., Chpt. 21). The implication is that there will be eating and drinking in this eternal city.

In the Garden of Eden the eating of the Tree of Life was a sacrament of fellowship with God and with life, a commemoration, a pledge, a support of and participation of life eternal, for soul and body. Sin, however, cut man off from that life, and all the Old Testament shadows and ordinances since that time are meant for man's recovery and readmission to that Tree. A Promise was given to the Church at Ephesus:

> *"To him who overcomes will I give to eat of the Tree of*

Life, which is in the midst of the Paradise of God" (Rev. 2:7).

Again we read:

> *"Blessed are they who do His Commandments, that they may have the right to the Tree of Life, and may enter in through the gates into the city"* (Rev. 22:14).

The leaves of the tree are also special, their purpose being a provision from God for preservation of natural life and eternal health.

The Promise to the overcomer is that there will be no more curse or evil, but the abiding Blessings of God's Presence and Glory. The glorified Saints will reign with God and Christ forever and ever in the new state. We will be with Him, we will serve Him, and we will . . .

> *"see His Face"* (Rev. 22:4).

What glory to behold Him face-to-face!

> *"And there shall be no more curse: but the Throne of God and of the Lamb shall be in it; and His Servants shall serve Him:*
> *"And they shall see His Face; and His Name shall be in their foreheads.*
> *"And there shall be no night there; and they need no candle, neither light of the sun; for the Lord God gives them Light: and they shall reign forever and ever"* (Rev. 22:3-5).

As the Apostle John saw and heard these wonderful things, he fell to worship at the feet of the Angel who spoke with him, but this messenger restrained him, declaring that he was also a fellow servant and one of his Brethren of the Prophets. The Angel exhorted John to *worship God.*

Then came the final instructions to God's Servant, reaffirming the soon Return of the Lord Jesus Christ in Glory.

> *"And, behold, I come quickly; and My reward is with Me, to give every man according as his work shall be.*
> *"I am Alpha and Omega, the Beginning and the End, the First and the Last.*
> *"I Jesus have sent My Angel to testify unto you these things in the Churches. I am the Root and the Offspring of David, and the Bright and Morning Star"* (Rev. 22:12-13, 16).

Knowing that these things that have been prophesied must come to pass . . .

> "*what manner of persons ought you to be in all Holy conversation and Godliness,*
> "*Looking for and hasting unto the coming of the Day of God . . .*" (II Pet. 3:11-12).

May we say, even as John:

> "*Even so, come, Lord Jesus*" (Rev. 22:20).